MELTDOWN

MELTDOWN

A Race Against Nuclear Disaster at Three Mile Island
A Reporter's Story

Wilborn Hampton

CANDLEWICK PRESS
CAMBRIDGE, MASSACHUSETTS

Library of Congress Cataloging-in-Publication Data

Hampton, Wilborn.
Meltdown: a race against nuclear disaster at Three Mile Island : a reporter's story/ by Wilborn Hampton.
p.   cm.
ISBN 0-7636-0715-0
1. Three Mile Island Nuclear Power Plant—Juvenile literature. 2. Nuclear power plants—
Accidents—Pennsylvania—Harrisburg Region—Juvenile literature.
3. Nuclear energy—Juvenile literature. [1. Three Mile Island Nuclear Power Plant.
2. Nuclear power plants—Accidents.] I. Title.
TK1345.H37 H36 2001
363.17'99'0974818—dc21   00-037959

2 4 6 8 10 9 7 5 3 1

Printed in Italy

This book was typeset in Melior.

Candlewick Press
2067 Massachusetts Avenue
Cambridge, Massachusetts 02140

visit us at www.candlewick.com

Also by Wilborn Hampton

Kennedy Assassinated! The World Mourns:
A Reporter's Story

C O N T E N T S

Part 1: Hiroshima

Chapter 1   3

Part 2: Three Mile Island

Chapter 2   15

Chapter 3   21

Chapter 4   29

Chapter 5   37

Chapter 6   41

Chapter 7   49

Chapter 8   57

Chapter 9   63

Chapter 10   69

Part 3: Chernobyl

Chapter 11   81

Acknowledgments   95

Glossary   97

Recommended resources   99

Bibliography   100

Index   101

Credits   103

HIROSHIMA

AUGUST 6, 1945

CHAPTER **1**

The atomic age began on July 16, 1945, near Alamogordo, New Mexico. A team of American scientists and reporters stood inside a bunker and watched the first atomic explosion erupt out of the desert in a blinding flash of light and form into a mushroom-shaped cloud.

That first test was part of the effort to bring an end to World War II by developing a powerful bomb that would use the enormous energy contained in the tiny atom. Those who witnessed that first explosion felt both the fear and hope the new energy held for mankind.

After watching the test, one of the scientists present said, "I am sure that on Doomsday, in the last millisecond, the last man on earth will see what we have just seen." But William Lawrence, a writer for the *New York Times*, said that he felt as though he had been present at the dawn of creation, when the Lord said, "Let there be light."

Page 2.
The first atomic explosion took place
near Alamogordo, New Mexico,
on July 16, 1945.

Three weeks after the test explosion in New Mexico, a group of B-29 bombers prepared to take off on a mission from the huge American air base on the island of Tinian, in the Pacific Ocean. One of those planes was to carry the special new atomic bomb that had just arrived from the United States. The pilot of the B-29 that was designated to drop this bomb had named the plane after his mother, Enola Gay. Even the bomb itself had a name. It was called Little Boy. Shortly before dawn on August 6, 1945, the *Enola Gay,* with Little Boy on board, took off. Its destination was Hiroshima, a city on the southwest coast of Japan.

The actual bomb run lasted four minutes. The only words entered in the copilot's diary were, "My God."

The bomb dropped on Hiroshima killed nearly 100,000 people instantly. Another 100,000 were severely wounded. This was out of a population of 245,000. More than 90 percent of the city was destroyed.

Three days later a second atomic bomb was dropped on the city of Nagasaki. Japan immediately offered an unconditional surrender, and World War II ended.

Survivors from the first bomb later said that all they remembered was a brilliant flash of blinding light, whiter than any white they had ever seen, exploding over Hiroshima. It was like millions upon millions of flashbulbs all going off at once. One person compared the blast to a giant sheet of sun being suddenly thrown over the city. Few recalled hearing any noise.

When an atomic bomb explodes, it creates a shock wave so powerful it can lift people standing over a mile away from the bomb site off the ground and hurl them through the air. This is followed by a wave of heat so tremendous it can start fires by spontaneous combustion and literally vaporize people if they are close enough.

When Little Boy exploded over Hiroshima, the entire city seemed to disintegrate. Glass, tile, wood, stone, concrete—all shattered into splinters. Buildings and houses collapsed into rubble. Fires suddenly erupted everywhere. It was estimated that the temperature at the point the bomb exploded exceeded

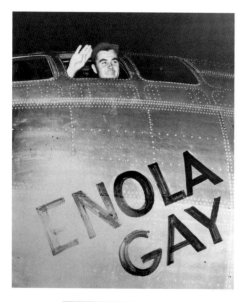

Col. Paul W. Tibbets, Jr., named the B-29 that carried the first atomic bomb after his mother.

10,000 degrees. Heat engulfed the city. Within minutes, the sky that had been so bright turned dark. As thousands of people wandered about the streets, dazed, burned, and bleeding, a giant cloud covered Hiroshima. The radioactive fallout had begun.

The anguish of the people of Hiroshima and Nagasaki was only beginning. Those who survived the initial blasts suffered horrible injuries and illnesses from the enormous amounts of radiation that fell on their cities during and following the explosions. And the end of the war did not bring an end to their suffering.

The atomic bombs that were dropped on Hiroshima and Nagasaki began a nightmare that went on for generations. For years, mothers gave birth to babies who were deformed—born without toes or fingers or with other genetic mutations. Thousands of people developed cancer or suffered from chronic radiation sickness. The radioactive fallout that blanketed the two cities seeped into the ground, polluting the water and contaminating any food grown there.

In the four minutes it took for the *Enola Gay* to drop an atomic bomb on Hiroshima the world became a much more terrifying place. A new force had been unleashed that carried with it the possibility of destroying the human race.

An escort plane photographed the deadly plume of smoke from the first atomic bomb as it rose 20,000 feet in the sky over Hiroshima, Japan.

Page 6, top.
A firestorm of suffocating smoke and blinding white heat engulfed Hiroshima, but there was no noise.

Page 6, bottom left.
Only one building and one tree survived the blast at ground zero where the bomb exploded.

Page 6, bottom right.
A pall of smoke hung over the ruins of the city one day after the explosion of the atomic bomb.

Page 7.
A Japanese soldier wandered through the rubble of Hiroshima. More than 100,000 people died instantly.

Because of its immense destructive power, the atomic bomb gave any country that had one an enormous threat to hold over its enemies, and so other nations rushed to develop bombs of their own. The Soviet Union successfully tested its first atomic weapon in 1949, and for the next forty years—during the ideological confrontation that came to be known as the Cold War—both the United States and the Soviet Union spent enormous amounts of money trying to build bigger and more deadly bombs. In 1952, America exploded a hydrogen bomb, in which a small conventional atomic bomb serves as the trigger for the fusion of hydrogen atoms, producing an even more massive explosion. The Soviet Union tested its own H-bomb a year later.

As the space age began, both sides began developing missiles that could deliver these nuclear bombs to targets thousands of miles away. Military commanders no longer needed airplanes like the B-29 to drop atomic bombs on one another's cities. All

Destruction at Hiroshima

The target for the *Enola Gay*'s mission was a district military headquarters located on an island in the middle of Hiroshima. The bomb actually exploded in the air more than a mile away, destroying buildings and setting fires within a radius of several miles from ground zero. The second bomb was dropped on Nagasaki.

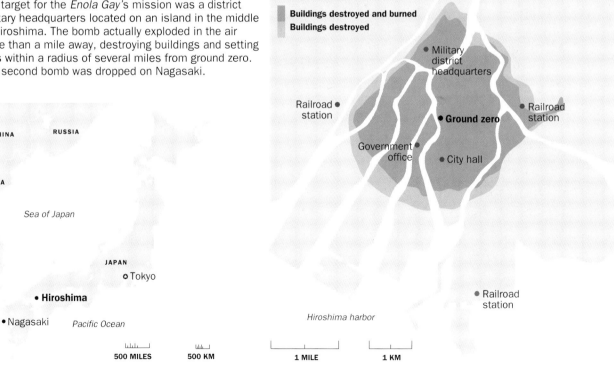

they had to do was push a button and a rocket would carry nuclear warheads halfway around the world to destroy entire cities and spread deadly radiation over hundreds of square miles.

The world learned to live in a sort of perpetual fear of nuclear holocaust. In the United States, schools held "civil defense" drills, much like fire drills, in which students and teachers practiced going to designated places in the basements of school buildings where they might be a bit safer during a nuclear attack. Some families built "fallout shelters" in their backyards. These were holes in the ground, covered by slabs of concrete that were supposed to protect people from radioactive fallout in the event of a nuclear attack. Shelters were also built in government buildings and other public places. Fortunately, they were never tested.

From the start, scientists believed that eventually atomic energy would be more of a blessing than a threat to mankind. The power released by splitting the atom could be constructive as well as destructive. All science had to do was to learn how to control it.

One peaceful application of the new technology was to use the energy and heat produced by an atomic reaction to generate power that would turn on lights in homes and operate machines in factories. Nuclear power could make electricity much more cheaply and cleanly than the traditional way of burning oil or coal. It was estimated that one ton of uranium—the raw material for nuclear power—could produce the same amount of energy as a million tons of coal. Nuclear power, it was said, would produce electricity that would be "too cheap to meter."

This was a strong argument in favor of nuclear power because the world that was emerging from World War II was going to need a lot of electricity. In the United States, especially, electrical appliances were vastly changing daily life. There were electric sweepers, dishwashers, and washing machines, freezers, air conditioners, stoves—even electric toothbrushes. All one had to do to achieve a better life was plug in the latest electrical

Americans, fearful of nuclear war in the decades following World War II, built fallout shelters in backyards and schools. This model on display in a department store showed the necessities for survival in case of nuclear attack.

Atomic energy was seen as the power of the future. Even stoves were expected to be operated by electricity generated by the atom.

Miniature atomic laboratories were popular children's toys. This one included radioactive material and a Geiger counter.

gadget. There was also a critical need for energy to bring light and modern communications to the poorer and less industrial nations of what we now call the developing world.

In addition to being cheap, nuclear energy was clean. There would be no more sooty black smoke billowing out of power plants, poisoning the very air that we breath. Finally, there was the simple necessity of finding new sources of energy for the future. Scientists were already warning that the world would soon run out of fossil fuels like coal, petroleum, and natural gas. The atom seemed to be the answer.

But from the beginning there were serious doubts about nuclear power. After all, the world's only experience with atomic energy so far had been in witnessing the devastating death and destruction it had caused in Hiroshima and Nagasaki. Even if it didn't produce harmful smoke like coal, the uranium fuel in nuclear plants would produce waste, and that waste would be radioactive. How would this nuclear waste be disposed of? And what if there was an accident at one of the plants?

What if one caught fire? What if the radiation from the uranium fuel escaped outside the plant? What if there was an explosion?

Supporters of atomic energy argued that the new nuclear power plants would have sophisticated safeguards built in that would shut them down in the event of an accident or a malfunction, and that so many backup protection devices would be in place that there would be no danger to the general population at all. As for the spent nuclear fuel, it could be reprocessed and used again, a sort of atomic recycling.

A national debate on the question of nuclear energy went on for several years, and even scientists and engineers were divided in their opinions. But as the memory of the horrors of Hiroshima faded with time, Americans grew more comfortable with the idea of nuclear energy.

The first nuclear power plant was built in Shippingport, Pennsylvania, and began operation in 1957. By 1974 there were forty-three licensed nuclear power plants throughout the United States, with another fifty-four under construction and fifty-three more on order to be built. A few small accidents had occurred at some of the plants, but they had presented no real danger to the general population. Slowly but surely it seemed that atomic energy was becoming part of the American way of life.

Then, one spring night in 1979, something happened at a place called Three Mile Island, in Pennsylvania, that rekindled all the fear Americans felt about nuclear power and reminded the world of the grim dangers inherent in the advent of the new atomic age.

THREE MILE ISLAND

MARCH 28 – APRIL 3, 1979

The first time I heard about Three Mile Island was on Friday morning, March 30, 1979, shortly after I arrived for work at the United Press International headquarters in New York. News agencies like U.P.I. and the Associated Press, then U.P.I.'s chief rival, provided news stories from around the world to newspapers and television and radio stations. At the time I was the editor in charge of U.P.I.'s foreign news report for the morning newspapers.

It was a desk job that I had taken over after returning from several years overseas as a foreign correspondent. I had joined U.P.I. straight out of college in 1963, in Dallas, Texas, and one of the first stories I covered was the assassination of President Kennedy. I sometimes missed being out in the field reporting on the big stories, but I also liked the regular hours of a desk job.

There wasn't a lot going on in foreign news at the time. The closest thing to a really big story in weeks had come on Wednesday, when the British prime minister, James Callaghan, lost a confidence vote in the House of Commons. As a result he would have to resign and ask Queen Elizabeth to call new elections. It was the first time in over fifty years that a British prime minister had been actually voted out of office by Parliament.

Wilborn Hampton covered the story of the nuclear accident at Three Mile Island in 1979 for United Press International.

Page 14.
Two nuclear reactors were built, Unit No. 1 in 1974 and Unit No. 2 in 1978, on an island in the middle of the Susquehanna River.

The candidate favored to win the next elections was the Conservative Party's leader, a woman named Margaret Thatcher. It was a pretty good story, but not what you would call earth-shattering.

I had been at work only a short time that morning when I had a call from H. L. Stevenson, the executive editor of U.P.I., whom everyone called Steve, to come into his office. Or rather I had a call from his secretary telling me to come to his office. That in itself was unusual. If Steve needed to talk to me personally about some particular story, he would just drop by my desk out in the newsroom. But most often he would confer with Walter Logan, who was the news agency's foreign editor, and Walter would pass on any instructions to me.

So I was more than a little curious why Steve would be calling me into his private office, and I really didn't know what to expect. I thought I should tell Walter that I had been summoned to see Steve. But when I walked over to inform him, he just nodded as though he already knew about it.

When I entered Steve's outer office, his secretary glanced up and said, "Go right on in. He's waiting for you."

"Have you been following this Three Mile Island thing?" Steve asked, motioning for me to sit in one of the two chairs in front of his desk. Steve was not one to waste a lot of time with preliminaries about the weather or "How are you?" or even "Good morning."

Radiation Is Released in Accident At Nuclear Plant in Pennsylvania

By DONALD JANSON
Special to The New York Times

MIDDLETOWN, Pa., Thursday, March 29 — An accident at a three-month-old nuclear power plant released above-normal levels of radiation into the central Pennsylvania countryside early yesterday.

By last night, officials of the Nuclear Regulatory Commission had still not determined the full extent of the radiation danger, but they said the amount of radiation that escaped was no threat to people in the area. Major amounts were released into the building housing the reactor, but workers were not believed to have been endangered.

Evacuation in Pennsylvania

The threat of a complete meltdown at Three Mile Island prompted the evacuation of many residents in towns near the nuclear reactor.

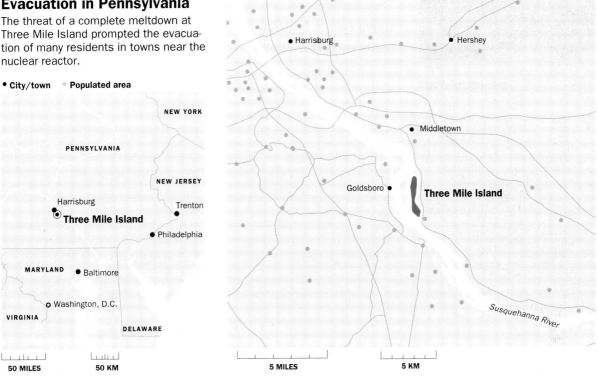

● City/town   ○ Populated area

NEW YORK

PENNSYLVANIA

NEW JERSEY

Harrisburg

Trenton

Three Mile Island

● Philadelphia

MARYLAND   ● Baltimore

○ Washington, D.C.

VIRGINIA

DELAWARE

50 MILES   50 KM

● Harrisburg   ● Hershey

● Middletown

Goldsboro ●   ●   Three Mile Island

Susquehanna River

5 MILES   5 KM

"Not closely," I replied, a little sheepishly. It was part of the job for any journalist to read as many newspapers and listen to as many newscasts as possible every day. A good news agency journalist knows what's going on anywhere around the world on any given day. But I had been running late getting to work that morning and had not turned on the radio or even looked at the papers. The truth was that I did not even know where Three Mile Island was. Was it some place in the Caribbean that had just declared its independence? Or maybe one of those islands in the South Pacific where the French were always conducting nuclear tests? My biggest fear was that there was some major foreign news story that we hadn't covered and I didn't even know about.

"It turns out to be worse than they first thought," Steve said.

"Oh, really?" I replied, trying to hide my ignorance.

As though he guessed, Steve shoved a copy of that morning's *New York Times* across his desk and pointed to the middle of the

Atomic Plant Is Still Emitting Radioactivity

By RICHARD D. LYONS
Special to The New York Times

MIDDLETOWN, Pa., Friday, March 30 — Radioactivity continued to leak from the crippled Three Mile Island atomic plant near here yesterday, and early today large amounts of water containing small amounts of radioactivity were released into the Susquehanna River to relieve pressure on the plant's holding tanks.

The 400,000 gallons of water contained small amounts of the radioactive gases xenon-133 and xenon-135. Federal nuclear safety officials said the gases posed little hazard to persons living downstream of the nuclear power plant.

'No Alternative,' Official Says

"There was no alternative — the tanks for holding such water were filling up," said Karl Abraham, a spokesman for the Nuclear Regulatory Commmission.

Yesterday, as the radioactivity seepage went on, nuclear power protesters flocked into the area and politicians demanded that steps be taken to insure public safety.

Detectable levels of increased radiation have spread over a four-county area, and officials of the utility that operates the almost-new generating plant said further discharges of radioactivity, such as iodine 131, would probably continue through today.

front page, to a headline that said, "Atomic Plant Is Still Emitting Radioactivity."

Curiously, I felt slightly relieved. At least I now knew what Steve was talking about. I had seen a story the previous day about an accident at a nuclear power plant in Pennsylvania that had released a small amount of radiation into the air. The reporter had quoted officials as saying the amount of radiation had been less than a person gets from a routine chest X-ray. I had not paid a great deal of attention to it. The follow-up story a day later, the one Steve was showing me now, said only that the plant was still leaking small amounts of radioactivity but this posed little danger to people living in the area.

I quickly read through it and looked back at Steve. I had no idea why he had called me into his office to discuss a story in Pennsylvania that at most seemed to be a minor local health concern. The British government had collapsed. We should be talking about our coverage of their upcoming elections. Had he forgotten that I worked on the foreign news desk? Pennsylvania was not a foreign country. This was national news.

"There have been developments," Steve said.

"What developments?" I asked.

"Do you know Bill Hoop?"

"Who?"

"He's been doing a great job. But he's going to need some help now."

Steve should have been a politician. He had a way of totally ignoring questions that was truly enviable. But I still did not know what he wanted from me.

"There's a flight to Philadelphia in a couple of hours," Steve said, as though no further explanation should be necessary. "You'll probably have time to get home and pack a shirt if you leave now."

It took a moment for what he was saying to sink in.

"You want me to help cover this story?"

"You can get a car at the airport in Philadelphia and drive over to Harrisburg."

"What are the 'developments'?" I persisted.

"Hoop will fill you in. The bureau is in the press office at the state capitol."

"But . . . What about . . . I don't . . ." I must have sputtered a few other things.

"You'll have to leave now, though, if you want to go home first," Steve said.

"Okay," I said. A good journalist also never turns down an assignment to cover a big news story, even if he doesn't know what it is. "I'll just go tell Walter. He'll have to find somebody to take over for me on the foreign desk."

"I'll tell Walter," Steve said. "You'd better get a move on."

As I raced home to pack a bag and get my portable type-writer, I thought about why Steve had called on me to help cover this story. During my time as a foreign correspondent, based in London and Rome, I had covered many big stories, from wars in the Middle East to disasters to diplomatic conferences. If he was wanting someone with experience at covering catastrophes, he must be expecting this Three Mile Island thing to be worse than it appeared.

The only problem was that I knew nothing about nuclear power plants. It was only after I was airborne, a couple of hours later, that it occurred to me that maybe I should have told Steve I had flunked physics in college.

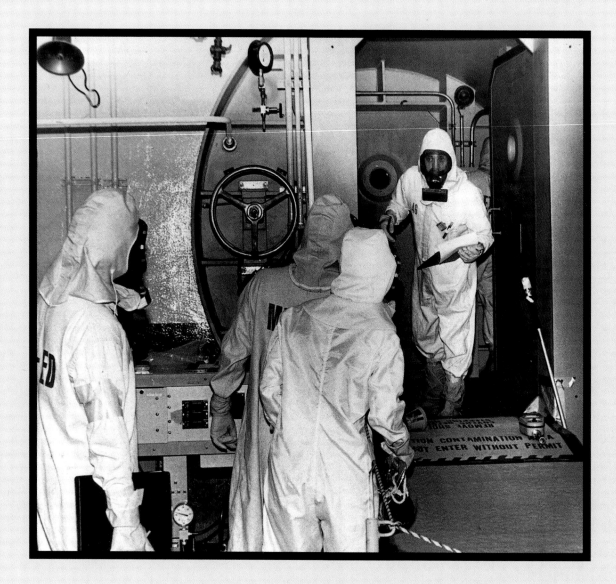

CHAPTER 3

The press office in the Pennsylvania state capitol in Harrisburg looked like a war room. There were dozens of reporters, all of whom looked urgently busy, either pounding away at typewriters or carrying on frantic telephone conversations with editors back at their newspapers. Paper cups half filled with cold, stale coffee were scattered here and there on their desks.

I found Bill Hoop and introduced myself. Hoop was the Harrisburg bureau manager, and as such he was the man in charge of the coverage of the Three Mile Island story. Although I had come from New York, which was U.P.I.'s world headquarters, he was the boss here and I was now working for him.

He was thin and wiry, as if maybe he had missed a few too many dinners chasing news stories. I figured him to be in his mid-thirties, a couple or three years younger than I was. He had a pleasant, boyish face surrounded by a shock of brown hair that probably never combed quite the way he wanted. I liked him on sight. He looked relieved to see me.

Although Harrisburg was the capital of Pennsylvania, it was a small city, and outside the state government not a lot happened that was of major interest to an international news agency. Hoop's job was mostly covering the governor and the Pennsylvania state legislature. When the Three Mile Island story first broke, Steve had sent Emil Sveilis, a reporter from U.P.I.'s closest large bureau, in Washington, D.C., over to Harrisburg to lend a hand in covering it. Now that the story was becoming even bigger, Hoop was looking for all the help he could get.

"There's going to be a news conference in a couple of hours," he said. "The bubble seems to be stable. They still haven't made a decision on an evacuation, though it doesn't look like they'll order one tonight."

"Bubble?" I asked. "Evacuation?"

"Let's go grab a bite to eat," Hoop said. "I'll fill you in over dinner. It's all been happening pretty fast."

My guess as to why he was so skinny appeared to be right. We went to a diner near the state capitol and both ordered the blue plate special. Since I had missed lunch, I was ravenous and mopped up everything on my plate. But Hoop just picked over his food while he told me why I suddenly found myself in rural Pennsylvania.

———

The trouble had started around 4 A.M. two days earlier, on Wednesday, March 28. Two workers named Craig Faust and Ed Frederick were nearing the end of what had been a quiet and uneventful overnight shift in the brand-new Unit No. 2 reactor at the Metropolitan Edison nuclear power plant at Three Mile Island, on the Susquehanna River. They had just carried out a routine check of the panels monitoring the reactor, and everything was working normally.

Suddenly warning lights began to flash in the control room and an alarm shrieked. Faust and Frederick raced to see what was wrong. Blinking red lights on one of the panels told them that two water pumps had failed. Without a constant flow of water to cool the reactor, heat was rapidly building up inside it.

This was a serious problem, but it was not a cause for panic. There was an emergency backup water flow built into the plant to take over in case of such malfunctions and keep the reactor cool. However, those first warning lights and siren were only the beginning of what became a dangerous situation in less than a minute.

Fifteen seconds after the primary water pumps failed, a valve became stuck in the open position. Radioactive steam and water began to spill into one of the reactor's tanks, draining off the water needed to cool the fuel rods in the core. Fifteen seconds after that, the emergency backup water system that would cool the unit failed because the maintenance crew that had gone off duty earlier had forgotten to open three other, hand-operated valves.

With water leaking out through the open valve and the emergency water flow being blocked by the closed valves, no water was reaching the fuel rods, which are supposed to be covered in water at all times. And no one in the control room realized the fuel rods were uncovered.

Faust and Frederick were racing around the control room trying to figure out from an array of hundreds of lights—red, green, white, blue, yellow, all blinking like a Christmas tree—what the main problem was and what they should do to fix it.

A lot more went wrong in very quick order. Between human error and equipment malfunctions, Three Mile Island was rapidly building into the worst nuclear crisis the country had ever faced. But in the first hours, the power company that owned the plant, Metropolitan Edison (known locally as Met Ed), failed to alert any state or federal official that anything was wrong, hoping that their technicians could fix whatever was going on inside the reactor.

It wasn't long before the technicians realized that radiation was leaking out of the reactor. Events were spinning out of control. Unit No. 2 was in big trouble.

Until the accident, the nuclear plant was a source of civic pride, and the public was invited to the observation deck.

One of the people Hoop had talked to on that first day was John Callahan, a construction worker at the plant. Callahan had come to work shortly after 6 A.M. that morning and had been admitted into Unit No. 2 as usual. No one told him that anything was wrong.

Callahan had been on the job for about half an hour when he and another worker noticed a puddle of water on the floor. There should not have been any water on the floor, and they were trying to figure out how it came to be there when one of the senior technicians came running through the building waving his hands and shouting, "Get out! Get your stuff and get out!"

The water Callahan had seen on the floor was radioactive.

By 7 A.M., it had become clear that not only was the alarming buildup of radiation escaping from the reactor but some of it might even be leaking outside the plant. They could not keep the accident a secret any longer.

Gary Miller was Met Ed's station manager for Three Mile Island. When he arrived in the control room at Unit No. 2, at approximately 7:15 A.M., there were about sixty people shouting and running back and forth as technicians tried to keep pace with the torrent of bad news coming from the instruments on the control panel.

Miller spent about five minutes listening to reports and studying data that confirmed fears that radiation levels were steadily increasing and radiation was spilling outside. At 7:24 A.M. he formally declared a "state of general emergency," the first ever at a nuclear power plant in the United States.

Met Ed finally began to telephone state and federal authorities to advise them of the situation. Even then, Met Ed tried to minimize the danger to the local population. As the governor, federal officials, and reporters began to ask questions about the emergency, Met Ed kept changing its story. At first spokesmen said it was a broken water pump, then a stuck valve, then a clogged filter. In fact, it was all of those things and a lot more.

Even as they were assuring Governor Dick Thornburgh and the Nuclear Regulatory Commission in Washington, D.C., that there was "no danger to public safety" from radioactive emissions, Met Ed officials knew that radioactive material was seeping outside the plant. They just didn't know how much.

Because of the radioactive water and gas within the containment building, no one was able to go back inside Unit No. 2 to make an assessment of the damage. All they had to go on was information transmitted from instruments that might have been damaged by the accident.

When Miller ordered readings taken on the amount of heat and the level of radiation that were building up inside the reactor, the results were so high—one showed that the temperature in the top of the reactor was over 4,000 degrees—that he thought the equipment was simply malfunctioning and so he discounted them.

Although the readings should have given the Met Ed technicians a clue as to the extent of the problem, no one considered the possibility that they were accurate—or that the incredibly high temperatures were the result of the fact that the fuel rods were no longer covered by water and were dangerously overheated.

———————

By the afternoon of that first day, Hoop told me, Met Ed had decided they had to get some reliable figures on the amount of radiation inside the building. Hoop then told me about Ed Houser.

Houser was the chief chemist for the Three Mile Island nuclear plant. Met Ed had called Houser in and told him he would have to go inside Unit No. 2 and take some radiation readings. Houser, who was married and had two children, was not happy about entering the building. But he knew the job had to be done.

For his assignment Houser wore three pairs of coveralls, three pairs of rubber gloves, a single pair of rubber boots, and a full-face respirator. All the clothing and rubber was supposed to protect him from radiation for a short period of time. His job was

Inside Three Mile Island 2

The reactor at Three Mile Island was a pressurized water reactor. Like runners in a relay race passing a baton, heated water from the core of the reactor flows through a generator, where it is turned into steam, then on to a turbine, which then produces electricity. As in any relay, the handoffs must be smooth and steady. If there is too little water at any point, the system fails because heat builds up at that point.

The primary cooling water, heated by the nuclear fuel but kept under extremely high pressure to keep it from turning into steam, is pumped up through the core. The secondary cooling water is kept in steel tanks. As the heated water from the core passes through it in thousands of small tubes, the secondary cooling water turns into steam, much like a radiator. The steam from the generators is piped into a turbine, where it spins the large turbine blades the way wind turns a windmill. The secondary cooling water is then pumped to the cooling tower before it is returned to the system.

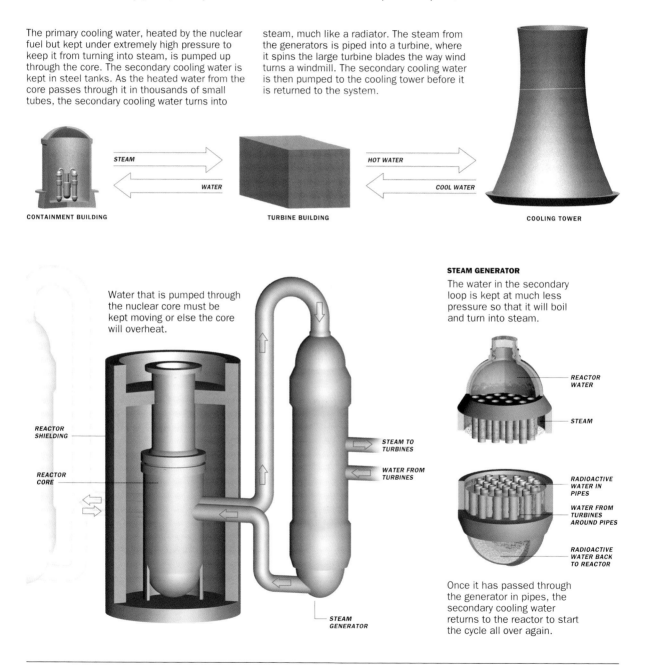

CONTAINMENT BUILDING

STEAM

WATER

TURBINE BUILDING

HOT WATER

COOL WATER

COOLING TOWER

Water that is pumped through the nuclear core must be kept moving or else the core will overheat.

REACTOR SHIELDING

REACTOR CORE

STEAM TO TURBINES

WATER FROM TURBINES

STEAM GENERATOR

STEAM GENERATOR

The water in the secondary loop is kept at much less pressure so that it will boil and turn into steam.

REACTOR WATER

STEAM

RADIOACTIVE WATER IN PIPES

WATER FROM TURBINES AROUND PIPES

RADIOACTIVE WATER BACK TO REACTOR

Once it has passed through the generator in pipes, the secondary cooling water returns to the reactor to start the cycle all over again.

to take a sample of the contaminated water on the floor of the building, take readings of the air inside the unit, and then get out.

At 4:30 P.M. on that first day, Houser walked into Unit No. 2 of the Three Mile Island nuclear plant. He stayed five minutes, then left hurriedly. While he was inside, he was bombarded with radiation from the water that by that time covered most of the floor, and by the "background" radiation that was bouncing off the walls of the containment building.

One standard measure of radiation is in units called rems. A routine chest X-ray, for example, is normally about 72 millirems, or 72 one-thousandths of a rem. The maximum radiation a human being should receive in a year is 5 rems. Houser reported that some of the readings he took inside the building were more than 1,000 rems an hour. If the level of radiation was that high in the containment building, it could be several times higher inside the reactor itself.

Despite Houser's findings, Met Ed officials issued a statement that the situation in the nuclear plant was "stable." But nothing the Met Ed officials could say would stop what was going on inside Unit No. 2. The crisis was just beginning.

Scientists and technicians in the control room of Unit No. 2 in the first days after the accident.

CHAPTER 4

The waitress came and took away our plates. Bill Hoop had barely touched his food while he filled me in on the background of the first two days. Now he told me what had happened on this, the third day, why the story had "suddenly gotten bigger," as Steve had put it. Why, in other words, I was there.

The bad news began early that morning, as most people in the surrounding towns were on their way to work. The amount of radioactivity that had continued to build up in the Three Mile Island plant for two days had increased dramatically during the night. Met Ed officials decided, without telling anyone, to release some of the excess radioactive steam into the air.

This release, or "venting" as scientists call it, was heard for miles around. In Middletown, the closest large town to Three Mile Island, people said it sounded like a jet plane revving for takeoff. People walking on the street, riding in their cars, standing in their kitchens at home heard a great whoosh and roar as a plume of radioactive steam spewed out of the crippled nuclear plant and into the atmosphere.

There was no hiding the danger any longer, or pretending it didn't really exist. One of the giant cement cooling towers that stood silently in the middle of the river, quietly menacing all who lived around it with its invisible terror, had suddenly burped into life with an eruption of deadly radiation that all could hear. And that was only the start of the day's surprises.

A short time later it was announced that a large hydrogen gas bubble had formed at the top of the nuclear reactor's core. Nobody seemed to know what caused it or why it was there, but it was blocking the flow of water that technicians were now pumping into the reactor in an attempt to cool the fuel rods. If the presence of the bubble allowed the tops of the fuel rods to overheat beyond a critical point, they would begin to melt.

Anyone who had been hoping that the plant could be brought under control through ordinary means now had to admit there was a very real danger of the thing everyone most feared. Dudley Thompson, an official from the Nuclear Regulatory Commission, held a briefing for reporters and laid it on the line: "We face the ultimate risk of a meltdown."

People who didn't know a rem from a gamma ray and thought a bubble was a kind of chewing gum knew the word "meltdown." For one thing, a movie called *The China Syndrome* had just been released, in which Jack Lemmon plays a scientist and Jane Fonda a television reporter who team up to expose the danger of a meltdown at a nuclear plant.

The title of the movie came from the popular misconception that in a nuclear meltdown the radioactive material would burn all the way through the earth to China. What would actually happen, as the movie explains, is that the molten fuel rods would quickly burn through the cement floor of the containment building and seep into the ground like a massive glob of fiery hot lava until it hit the water table, at which point it would not only contaminate the surrounding countryside, but geysers of radioactive steam would shoot back up into the atmosphere and form into radioactive clouds that would travel whichever way the wind blew.

It had never happened, so no one knew exactly how devastating a meltdown could be. But a government study in 1975 had estimated that a meltdown in a moderately populated area could kill over 3,000 people immediately and cause 45,000 cases of radiation sickness. But the disaster would not end there. The study further estimated that within a few years an extra 45,000 people would die from cancer, and that there would be 5,000 cases of genetic birth defects within the first generation after a meltdown.

According to Hoop, things had started happening very quickly after that. Both the state and federal governments had lost patience with Met Ed. And if the residents in the towns around Three Mile Island had been uneasy over the past couple of days, they were now just plain scared. And they wanted some action.

Experts agreed that if there was a serious danger of a meltdown, or even of more uncontrolled releases of radioactive gas, residents should be moved away from the entire area. President Jimmy Carter ordered the Defense Department to draw up evacuation plans for all surrounding towns. He also ordered Harold Denton, a top official with the Nuclear Regulatory Commission, to go to Harrisburg as his personal representative.

With the threat of a meltdown now out in the open, the Pennsylvania state government in Harrisburg had to act. As the

An antinuclear demonstrator protested in front of a theater showing a popular movie about a meltdown at a nuclear plant.

U.S. AIDES SEE A RISK OF MELTDOWN AT PENNSYLVANIA NUCLEAR PLANT; MORE RADIOACTIVE GAS IS RELEASED

CHILDREN EVACUATED

But Governor Says Later Further Pullouts Are Not Thought Likely

By RICHARD D. LYONS
Special to The New York Times

MIDDLETOWN, Pa., March 30 — Gov. Dick Thornburgh advised pregnant women and small children today to stay at least five miles away from the crippled Three Mile Island nuclear power plant as radioactivity continued to leak and another burst of contaminated steam had to be released for safety reasons.

Tonight, at a Harrisburg news conference, Government nuclear experts said there was no immediate threat to public health, but Governor Thornburgh said his suggestion for the women and children "remains in force until tomorrow."

Earlier in the day several thousand schoolchildren were evacuated from the plant area, 10 miles southeast of Harrisburg, and other people began leaving on the Governor's advice. More than 150 pregnant women and young children were at a shelter in Hershey, for example.

bad news kept piling up, Governor Thornburgh called two news conferences in the space of two hours. What he said in them did nothing to ease people's minds.

At the first briefing, at about 10 A.M., the governor warned everyone living within ten miles of the plant to stay indoors until midnight that night. Sound trucks started cruising the streets of all the towns in the area warning people over loudspeakers not to leave their homes. At about noon, the governor issued a new advisory for all pregnant women and all schoolchildren—the people most susceptible to harm from radiation—within a five-mile radius of the nuclear plant to leave the area until further notice.

The governor also ordered the closing of all schools within a ten-mile radius of Three Mile Island. Emergency centers were quickly set up in school gymnasiums and in churches in neighboring counties to take in evacuees. Twenty-three schools in the area were closed. Thousands of schoolchildren were suddenly herded into cafeterias and auditoriums to wait for buses to drive them to evacuation centers more than twenty miles away.

This action only added to the general confusion. Parents, many of whom were now preparing to leave the area themselves, did not know where their children were. School officials started calling parents to tell them that their children had been evacuated. In some cases the schools didn't know where their students had been taken.

But that was only the start of the chaos. Many residents decided that they had heard enough, and an exodus of ordinary citizens began from the towns near the nuclear plant. In a matter of hours, southern Pennsylvania took on the aspect of a war zone, complete with long lines of refugees, as tens of thousands of people departed on their own without waiting for an official evacuation order.

Many people simply walked out of their houses, got into their cars, and drove off to towns twenty or thirty or a hundred miles away. Some left their front doors open and their television sets on in their haste to get away. Looting of houses that had been left open or unlocked by frightened residents became an immediate concern, and police forces were put on alert in all the surrounding towns. All police leaves and vacations were canceled.

The prospect of packing up and leaving their homes because of some invisible yet horrifying danger became the main preoccupation for most of the residents of towns around Three Mile Island, from Middletown to Harrisburg. Instead of the usual greetings of "How are you?" friends that Friday asked one another, "Are you going to leave?" or "Where are you going?" People inquired about the latest radiation count, which the radio was broadcasting every hour, the way they might normally ask if they thought it would rain. What the actual radiation count was depended on whom you listened to.

Scores of businesses and shops in both Middletown and Harrisburg simply closed and sent their employees home. Half the downtown area of Middletown was empty by Friday afternoon, and there were long lines at gas stations as people waited to fill up the tanks of their cars just in case there was an order to evacuate. Some service stations took advantage of the panic and immediately raised their gas prices.

Grocery stores around Middletown were running out of certain items, especially canned goods, because so many people

In the hours after the accident, civilian defense workers measured levels of radiation at key points around the region.

Homes, schools, and businesses surrounded the Three Mile Island plant.

were stocking up on food to take with them in the event of an evacuation. And there were already reports that some truck drivers were refusing to make deliveries of groceries and other goods into the area out of fear of radioactivity.

———

It was nearly time for the evening briefing. We got the bill and paid it. It seemed unlikely to me that any major development would come out of the news conference. It had been my experience that major news, certainly anything like a general evacuation of hundreds of thousands of people from their homes, is rarely kept secret until it can be announced at a news conference that has been scheduled for hours. If such an evacuation became necessary, it would begin immediately and the governor would announce it within minutes of making the decision.

I could sense Hoop was anxious about something, so I told him my theory to ease his mind. But something else was troubling him.

"You have children?" he asked.

"A boy," I said. "But he lives with his mother. We're divorced."

Hoop just nodded. We walked a bit farther. Then he spoke again.

"If it comes to a meltdown or an evacuation," he said, "I want you to know I don't expect you to stay. You should get the hell out. I told Sveilis the same thing."

We were walking side by side toward the capitol. I glanced at him. His head was down and he was staring at the sidewalk. I didn't know whether Hoop and Sveilis were married or had children. I didn't ask. I pictured my son, who was then ten, briefly in my mind. But there was no question about what I had to do.

"If it comes to a meltdown or an evacuation," I replied, "I'll stay here and we'll cover it and then when everybody else is gone, we'll both get the hell out of town as fast as we can."

Hoop nodded and we walked on to the news conference in silence.

CHAPTER 5

As I had guessed, no major announcements were made at the news conference that night. Although the press conference had been called by Governor Thornburgh, the main attraction was Harold Denton, the man President Carter had sent to take over the crisis at Three Mile Island.

At the time, Denton, whose job was overseeing the regulation of the nation's nuclear reactors, was unknown outside his own circle. His picture had not been on television or on the cover of news magazines. He was a scientist, not a politician, and he was not used to holding nationally televised news conferences. Within the next few days, his name would be known in virtually every household in America.

I was impressed with Denton from the start. He had a sort of boy-next-door face, with a lock of hair that fell across his forehead. But it was also a face that one felt instinctively one could trust. And that was going to be a critical factor in trying to win the confidence of a population and a press corps that had grown distrustful because of the contradictions they had heard about the accident at Three Mile Island for two days.

The governor spoke first. He had good news and bad news. First he said that his advisory that everyone within ten miles of the plant should

Harold Denton, Director of Operations for the Nuclear Regulatory Commission, and Governor Dick Thornburgh brief reporters.

stay indoors would expire at midnight. But he also extended his order that all children and pregnant women stay away from the area for another day.

Then Denton took over. He didn't try to cover up the grim facts facing the residents of southeastern Pennsylvania. The hydrogen bubble was there, he said, and nobody knew how to get rid of it because it was not a problem that had ever arisen before. Because of the bubble, he explained, the tops of the fuel rods were exposed and overheating. He said that while there was a possibility of a meltdown, it was "very remote." And he said that the scientists had several days to figure out what to do about it.

Whether what Denton said was true, or whether it was just more of the same old razzle-dazzle Met Ed had spouted when the crisis first broke remained to be seen. But for some reason he convinced me that he knew what he was talking about, and I felt I could believe him.

After the news conference, we went into the press room and I waited while Hoop wrote a story. On the way out, Hoop handed me a glossy booklet about the Three Mile Island plant that the Met Ed people had distributed to journalists.

"Nuclear physics 101," he said. "This is supposed to explain how it works. They handed these out the first day."

———————

In my rental car I followed Hoop to the motel on the edge of Harrisburg where I was staying. I had not even checked in. We went into the lounge to discuss the coverage for the following day.

I had already been thinking about the problems we were going to face covering this story, as I'm sure Hoop had. The first and foremost of these was that there wasn't any real hard news to report. This story was going to get banner headlines in newspapers around the world starting tomorrow morning, but as of that moment it was a breaking news story on which nothing was breaking. There was a bubble in a nuclear reactor that might cause a disaster, and a plan had been drawn up to evacuate the entire surrounding countryside. But until those things

Page 36.
The top portion of Unit No. 1 at Three Mile Island. It was the top of Unit No. 2 in which a hydrogen bubble formed following the accident.

happened—and everybody hoped they wouldn't—reporters would be playing a waiting game along with the scientists.

Reporters trying to cover this story found themselves in a similar situation to the scientists—it was something none of us had ever faced before. There had been no story like it to use as a guideline. I thought the best way to approach it was the same way one covered a disaster story. On disaster stories, you report what has happened—a hurricane, flood, tornado, earthquake, riot, war. We describe the damage and interview the survivors, who provide the eyewitness details that bring home the drama of what people have endured to readers and viewers far away. With television, of course, there is also film of the destruction. At Three Mile Island, there were no "survivors," no devastation to film, and as yet no disaster. This was going to be like covering a disaster—except this would be a disaster before it happened instead of after.

I asked Hoop what town was closest to the stricken nuclear plant. He said that while Middletown was the largest nearby town, there was a smaller one named Goldsboro on the other side of the river that was closer. I told him I would like to go over there and look around. He thought this was a good plan and we agreed to meet up the following afternoon in Middletown.

It was around 11 P.M. by the time I got into bed. It had been a long day, one that began with my sitting in New York wondering how we were going to cover the British elections and was now ending with my sitting in a motel in Harrisburg, Pennsylvania, trying to figure out whether a hydrogen bubble in a nuclear power plant could cause a meltdown, or force nearly a quarter of a million people out of their homes.

I decided to study the Met Ed booklet. I looked at the drawings of the fuel rods and control rods and water inflow and outflow and steam generators, and I was asleep in about two minutes flat. The first thing I saw as I reached for the phone when my wakeup call came the next morning was a sketch of a nuclear power plant in the booklet that lay open on the side of the bed.

CHAPTER 6

As the crow flies, Goldsboro is only about four miles from Middletown. But there is no bridge along that particular stretch of the Susquehanna, so I had to drive about twenty miles north before I could cross to the other side. From that distance, the huge cooling towers of the nuclear plant looked less forbidding. But as I drove back toward Goldsboro on the other side of the river, they slowly began to loom large again.

It was a sunny, pleasant day, warm for late March, and I had the windows of the car rolled down as I drove. I didn't have any particular plan once I got to Goldsboro. I thought I would just try to talk to some of the residents and get some sort of feel for what it was like to live in the shadow of a nuclear plant.

As I turned off the highway to drive into the town, the towers appeared to rise up out of the river, like the turrets on some evil castle, dwarfing the town. Only a narrow stretch of water separated Three Mile Island from Goldsboro, and the nuclear plant itself was less than half a mile away.

I didn't know how many people in Goldsboro had already left town on their own. Perhaps the residents would be reluctant to discuss the accident and what they thought about the nuclear plant. Fear often makes people

Page 40.
Goldsboro, located less than half a mile from the nuclear plant across the Susquehanna River, was like a ghost town in the days following the accident.

reticent to talk, especially to strangers. They begin to think that all outsiders are the enemy. In fact, I really didn't know what to expect when I reached Goldsboro. But I certainly didn't expect what I found. The place was like a ghost town. The only thing that was missing were the tumbleweeds.

It was a neat little town with streets of white frame houses and well-tended front lawns. But as I drove slowly into its center, I saw nothing but house after house with front doors closed, windows shut, and curtains drawn. There was not another car on the main street.

I drove past Reeser's grocery store and Hartman's beauty shop. The doors on both were shut with a "Closed" sign on the front. I drove past a filling station, but there were no cars there and locks had been attached to the gas pumps. I drove past the local post office, but even it was closed. I drove past one house that had a sign in the front yard that said "Worms for Sale," but someone had written the word "Closed" on a piece of cardboard and tacked it to the bottom.

It was one of the eeriest feelings I had ever had in my life. I felt as though I had driven onto the set of a horror movie about a town that had been wiped out by the plague or pod people or something. There was no immediate sign of life to be seen.

I pulled the car over to the curb and turned off the ignition. I looked across the river at those towers and thought about the situation. There was a real danger here. But of what? This was not a threat you could see. There was no black funnel knifing out of the sky, no wall of water cascading through the street, no sniper on a roof shooting at people. Yet the sense of menace was no less tangible for its being invisible. It was everywhere, even in the very air I was breathing. The more I thought about it, the more nervous I became myself.

As I considered the unknown dangers lurking outside, I suddenly felt I should take some kind of precaution. So I reached over and quickly rolled up all the windows in the car.

After sitting there for three or four minutes, sweating but feeling a bit safer, a light bulb went off in my head, and I realized how totally useless that gesture was. The radiation, of course, was invisible, and it could be in the very air I was breathing. Car windows were not going to protect me.

I decided to take a stroll around town. I rolled the windows back down and got out of the car. There didn't seem to be much point in locking it. There was nobody around to steal it anyway.

Despite the fact that no one was on the street, I was fairly sure the entire town had not simply fled. I walked up the main street and knocked on several doors. No one answered. Then I noticed

Some residents didn't wait for an evacuation order and simply packed a suitcase and left.

one house across the street with its front door open. I knocked there. Again there was no response, but I decided to try the back-yard. Sure enough, there was a man at the back of the house in a small shed.

Ron Jones, a retired man in his sixties who said he did some volunteer work with the local civil defense, told me a few people started leaving the first day of the accident but most had gone the day before, right after Met Ed vented the giant plume of radiation. He estimated that about three-fourths of the town's population of 620 had left.

"I would have gone, too," Jones said. "But I didn't have any place to go."

I asked him what he was doing. He said he was getting ready to plant his spring garden vegetables, but he didn't know whether it would be safe to eat them if they kept releasing radiation from the plant.

Jones said he was listening to all the news broadcasts in case there was an evacuation order. I asked him what he would do then if he didn't have any place to go.

"Oh, I won't go anywhere," he said. "But they'll need some help from the civil defense if they order a general evacuation."

He sounded almost hopeful that one would be ordered.

Back on the main street, I walked toward the river. A rail line ran alongside the Susquehanna at the far end of the town. As I approached it I saw another man standing at the crossing where the railroad intersected with the street. He was staring up at the nuclear plant just across the water.

Woodrow Miller had been Goldsboro's mayor until he was defeated in the last election.

"I've lived here all my life," Miller said. "I'm not about to leave now."

Miller reminisced about his boyhood in the town, when he used to hunt for arrowheads on the island not much more than a strong stone's throw away, where the giant towers now stood. He said no one in the town had opposed the construction of the nuclear plant when it was first proposed. It brought employment to the town, and most people had believed it would produce cheaper power and would be safe. But he said the accident had changed a lot of residents' minds.

"They were all for it until this," he said. "I never heard a word against that plant in this town until now. They changed their minds overnight. Now they're all against it."

Miller said there had been a bigger debate over the railroad that ran through the town than over the nuclear plant. He said the railway had been a major health concern, too, because of the cargo that was transported on it.

"When I was mayor we used to fight that railway all the time," he said. "They carried everything through this town—all kinds of dangerous chemicals—and we were worried about a derailment. We never thought about any problems from the nuclear plant."

Asked if he would stay in Goldsboro through the crisis no matter what happened, Miller thought a moment and said, "Well, if the radiation did get a lot higher . . . certainly. I'd leave. I'm not going to stay here and die. But until they say it's a lot worse than it is now, I'm going to stay right here."

As I walked back to my car I noticed that a television sound truck had pulled up on the opposite side of the street, and a man in a suit and tie was walking toward me along the sidewalk. Behind him, near the truck, were two more men in jeans, one of whom was cradling a portable television camera. The other one was probably a sound engineer. The suit and tie called out to me.

"Is that your car?"

I replied that it was.

"Could you move it? We're trying to get a picture of the empty street."

I crossed the street and got into the car. As I turned on the ignition, I saw the TV reporter, now holding a microphone, positioning himself on the sidewalk while the cameraman focused in on him. It appeared he was getting ready to do a "stand-upper," which is TV jargon for a filmed report from the scene in which the correspondent simply stands up in front of the camera and delivers his report. This one would be from a deserted street with the Three Mile Island towers in the background.

As I looked in my rearview mirror before pulling away from the curb, I noticed another television truck pull around the corner and drive slowly down the street. The first TV reporter gave a "cut" motion to his cameraman and waited for the offending rival vehicle to move out of camera range.

But the second unit eased over to the curb and parked just ahead of the waiting reporter, and its crew got out on the sidewalk. As I pulled into a driveway to turn around and head out of town, I overheard the first reporter complaining to the new arrivals, "I can't film a ghost town with a mobile unit in the background."

I didn't stay to see how it turned out.

———————

By the time I got back to Middletown, the telephone company was busy installing phones inside a press center that had been set up on the basketball court of a youth center in the town hall. Hundreds of reporters were milling about. Just about every major newspaper had sent its own reporter to the scene, and in addition to all the American television networks there were crews from England, France, and other countries around the world.

Workers at Three Mile Island were checked for radiation before being allowed to leave the plant.

There seemed to be more journalists than local residents in Middletown.

At the entrance to the press center there was a table with a sign advising all reporters to pick up dosimeters to wear while out covering the story. Dosimeters are little instruments that are supposed to measure the amount of radiation to which a person has been exposed. I decided not to get one. I figured that if I was absorbing dangerous amounts of radiation it was something I'd rather not know about.

I sat on one end of a bench outside the press center, searching for Hoop or Sveilis in the crowd of reporters and looking over my notes from my trip to Goldsboro. Suddenly I saw a television newswoman, microphone in hand, with a cameraman and sound technician behind her, approach a woman sitting on the other end of the bench.

The reporter addressed the woman on the bench.

"Excuse me, but I see you have made a decision to stay in town?"

"Yeah," the other woman said. "I guess I'm here for the duration."

"Does that mean you still won't leave even if an evacuation is ordered?"

"I don't know."

"So you haven't made up your mind?"

"Well, it depends on what my editor tells me to do."

It turned out the woman on the bench was a reporter too.

I decided to look for Hoop inside the press center. It was crowded and I stood near the entrance looking out over all the reporters talking on telephones, scribbling on notepads, asking each other questions. Suddenly a man was at my side. He was slightly out of breath and looked like he had just gotten off an airplane that he had run to catch. When he spoke it was with a heavy German accent.

"Please to tell me," he asked. "Is the total evacuation finished?"

I assured him there had been no evacuation except for pregnant women and young children and motioned to the hundred or so reporters in the press center as if to prove my point.

"Ach," he said, visibly relieved. "Then I have arrived in time to be evacuated."

I heard someone call my name and turned to see Hoop and Sveilis both just outside the center's entrance. I went out to join them. They were standing near the table where journalists were lined up to register to get their dosimeters.

"Did you get one of those?" Hoop asked, nodding to the table.

"No. I figure if I start to glow you and Emil will let me know."

Hoop told me that Steve had sent some reinforcements to help with U.P.I.'s coverage. Ed DeLong, a science reporter, had arrived from Washington to handle the technical side of the story, along with two other reporters, Bob Grotevant and Scott MacLeod. I asked Hoop if there had been any developments with the bubble. He said Denton was going to hold a news conference that evening.

CHAPTER 7

From the start, the crisis at Three Mile Island was a race against time: would the scientists be able to eliminate the hydrogen bubble in the top of the reactor before the exposed fuel rods reached the critical heat that would trigger a meltdown? The problem was that nobody knew how much time they had.

Harold Denton believed scientists had days to try to get rid of the bubble and cover the tops of the fuel rods with water before a meltdown would begin. Other experts feared they didn't have that luxury and that a meltdown could happen at any time. The debate was of more than scientific interest.

The key concern, of course, was the safety of the more than 200,000 people who lived in towns around the plant. Officials couldn't just wait for a meltdown to begin and then hope to conduct an orderly evacuation of all the residents who might be in the path of the inevitable radioactive cloud. On the other hand, you can't just order hundreds of thousands of people to abandon their homes, possibly never to return, on a whim.

The question of whether to order a full evacuation had turned into a major dispute between the scientists in Washington and those on Three Mile Island. They all were working with the same information, but they were reaching different conclusions.

Page 48.
Fearful residents followed every development in the crisis. Those who had left the area waited for word that it was safe to return home.

In the foreground: Harold Denton, Roger Mattson, Director of the NRC's Division of Systems Safety, and Joseph Fouchard, NRC's public affairs director.

Roger Mattson, a government scientist whose analysis of the data being issued at the crippled plant had revealed the existence of the hydrogen bubble in the top of the reactor vessel, was a leading advocate in favor of an evacuation. By now the scientists knew that the fuel rods in Unit No. 2 had been uncovered during the early part of the accident and that some of the rods had begun to crack open from the massive heat. Mattson had also discovered from old data that there had been a small explosion inside the containment vessel on the first day of the accident; no one had known about it at the time because the computer printouts had run so far behind the events as they were happening.

Mattson believed that little time remained before a meltdown occurred. He compared the effort to get rid of the bubble before it began as a "horse race." At one point in the debate he advised members of the Nuclear Regulatory Commission, "We have got an accident that is deteriorating slowly, and is on the threshold of turning bad. And I don't have a reason for not moving people. I don't know what you are protecting by not moving people."

Denton and his team at the plant agreed that the critical question was time, but he believed, as he had said several times, "Time is on our side."

The final decision on an evacuation would rest with Governor Thornburgh, and the governor was relying on the N.R.C. chairman, Joseph M. Hendrie, for advice. To be fair, neither side had much solid information to go on. At one point, Hendrie said that he and Governor Thornburgh had so few hard facts on which to base a decision that they were "like a couple of blind men staggering around."

A key factor in the argument over whether or not to evacuate was how much time there would be between the point scientists knew for sure there would be a meltdown and when it actually started.

The estimate was that there would be between six to twelve hours from the time there was nothing left to do—no more switches to press or pull, no more water to pump—and they could only let the melting nuclear fuel run its course. They figured that it would then take three or four hours for the radioactive fuel to work its way through the containment vessel. That didn't leave a lot of time to get 200,000 people out of town.

As reporters learned later, Hendrie was asked, during one of the endless discussions the commissioners had on this subject, if there was anything that could happen that would leave them with less time than that to evacuate the area.

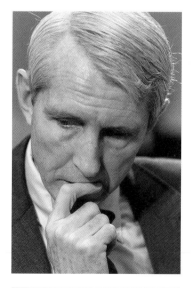

Hendrie replied that while it was highly unlikely, there was one thing that couldn't be ruled out.

"What would that be?" he was asked.

"A hydrogen explosion," he replied.

No one knew exactly what would happen if there was an explosion in Unit No. 2 at Three Mile Island. It would not be the enormous kind of explosion made by a hydrogen bomb. But the catastrophe would be no less devastating since it would spew large amounts of radioactive material into the air. And it would leave a good part of southern Pennsylvania uninhabitable for a very long time.

Joseph M. Hendrie, NRC chairman.

In his dealings with the press and media, Denton always tried to be straightforward and helpful. Since few journalists understood much about nuclear physics, he had to explain the same things over and over. But he was always patient and mild-mannered, and he never talked down to the reporters. He was fast winning the respect of the press corps covering Three Mile Island.

There was little news at the evening briefing. Denton said the situation inside the reactor had not changed. Although the bubble was no bigger, it was no smaller either. And until it went away completely and allowed the scientists to cool the reactor completely, the risk of a meltdown was still very real. But he reiterated that they had days to achieve this. He then went over a lot of old ground for the benefit of all the new reporters who had arrived during the day. I didn't mind the repetition, particularly since I was still struggling to understand what was happening inside the crippled reactor.

As near as I could figure out, what was going on in Unit No. 2 was somewhat similar to what happens when a bottle of soda sits in the sun, or you shake it up and hold your thumb on top. To keep the soda from spewing out you have to let it cool off or remove your thumb slowly to let the gas escape gradually. Another analogy is what happens when a car overheats. If you suddenly take the cap off the radiator without first letting the engine cool down, a geyser of hot water and steam will shoot out. Of course, the consequences facing Denton and the other scientists at Three Mile Island were not spraying the countryside with hot soda pop or even scalding water, but deadly radiation.

Denton repeated for the benefit of all the new reporters that the appearance of the bubble in the top of the reactor was a whole new development. Scientists had simply never faced it before, had never even contemplated such a problem, and they weren't sure how to get rid of it. He said they were trying to reduce the size of the bubble, which was estimated to be about 1,000 cubic feet, by pumping water into the reactor's core and venting some of the radioactive gas that had built up inside.

Threat of a meltdown

The accident at Three Mile Island began when the flow of water in the reactor was interrupted. Deprived of cooling water, the fuel rods in the reactor began to overheat. An emergency pump kicked in to speed the flow of cooling water to the core. But a gauge indicated that there was already enough water in the core so technicians turned it off. What technicians did not know was that an open valve was draining water from the reactor. In addition, backup pumps in the secondary loop were automatically turned on. But two cutoff valves had been left closed, preventing that water from reaching the core. Steam and hydrogen and radioactive gases began to build up in the core. The rods began to melt.

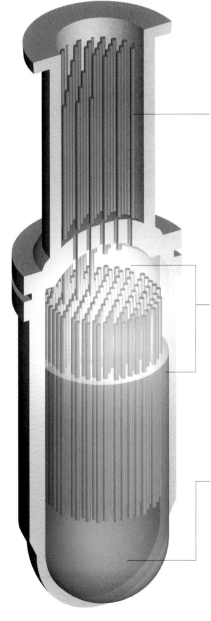

What went wrong

With the 12-foot-long fuel rods — the metal rods holding the uranium pellets that provide the nuclear reaction — left uncovered by water, they began to overheat, going from a normal 600 degrees to over 4,000 degrees. Radio-activity levels soared inside the reactor containment building.

A hydrogen bubble developed in the reactor, growing in size and raising fears among some scientists of an explosion that would release radioactivity into the air. The bubble also kept cool-ing water from reaching the fuel rods, and they continued to melt. The control rods, which act as a sort of dimmer switch by slowing the fission process when inserted between the fuel rods, were low-ered, but they could not stop the nuclear reaction.

As the tops of the fuel rods began to melt, the radioactive material dripped into the bottom of the reactor, which was encased in a 40-foot-high steel structure. If enough of the nuclear core melted, it would eat through the cement floor of the containment building.

Worst case scenarios

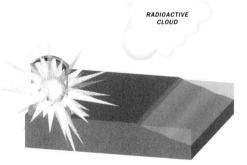

RADIOACTIVE GEYSERS

RIVER

ISLAND

GROUNDWATER

If the molten fuel had burned through the cement floor of the building, it would have seeped into the ground until it hit water, instantly turning the water into steam and shooting streams of radioactive geysers back up into the air, in parking lots, roads, and fields in the surrounding area.

RADIOACTIVE CLOUD

An explosion could have blown the top off the reactor and released clouds of radioactive gas into the air, to be carried whichever way the wind blew. Such an explosion would not, however, have been like that caused by an atomic bomb.

Slowly letting the thumb off the soda bottle, I thought.

After the conference we went back to the bureau in the state capitol and while Hoop filed a story based on Denton's news conference, I read through the newswire reports to find out what else was going on in the world. There were stories from all over the country about demonstrators holding "die-in's" and protest marches against nuclear energy. I noticed that none of these groups were coming to Middletown itself to demonstrate.

After Hoop finished we all went to a hotel near the capitol to get a bite to eat and discuss the next day's coverage. The bar was packed two-deep in journalists from all over the country, swapping rumors and speculation.

We took a table in the restaurant and ordered. Since the next day was a Sunday, it occurred to me that there might be a story in trying to cover some of the church services in Middletown—see how many people showed up, what the preachers said in their sermons. What does a pastor say to his flock facing possible nuclear disaster? Hoop, Emil, Scott, Bob, and I all divided up which church services we would each attend.

As we were leaving the restaurant I noticed a small blackboard at one end of the bar, on which the next day's weather forecast was usually chalked. Some wag had written, "Sunny with a high of 3,000 degrees."

Humor is always welcome.

CHAPTER 8

Another debate broke out that Saturday, and this one had even more dangerous implications. When the hydrogen bubble was first discovered in the reactor, no one gave much thought to the possibility that it might cause an explosion. Hydrogen by itself does not explode. It has to be mixed with oxygen before it becomes explosive. And as far as anyone knew, there was no oxygen in the reactor.

But there was water, and the water was radioactive. Scientists in Washington became concerned that because of all the radioactivity a chemical process known as radiolysis—in which the hydrogen and oxygen that combine to make water become separated—might be taking place. If that were the case, then pure oxygen was being created inside the reactor, and if enough of it mixed with the hydrogen bubble the reactor could catch on fire and eventually explode.

It was this possibility that had prompted Hendrie to warn about the one scenario in which there would be less than six hours to make a decision on any evacuation.

The team of government scientists in Washington set about trying to figure out how much oxygen was inside the reactor. The first calculations showed about 3 percent oxygen, and that the oxygen level would have to reach 8 or 9 percent before the hydrogen became flammable and 10 or 12

Page 56.
Visitors were no longer welcome at
the Three Mile Island plant after
the accident.

percent before it became explosive. They also figured that the oxygen was increasing at a rate of about 1 percent a day, so it would be days before the oxygen reached a critical level.

But as the Washington scientists kept crunching numbers, the prognosis changed. By late Saturday, Roger Mattson was convinced that there was now 5 percent oxygen in the reactor instead of 3 percent, and that instead of needing to reach 8 or 9 percent, the hydrogen could become flammable at 5 percent oxygen. As Mattson saw it, the reactor could burst into flames at any moment.

Denton's team of scientists back at Three Mile Island came to a different conclusion. Victor Stello, Denton's chief engineer, was working with the same figures as Mattson, but he believed that there was no danger at all of the reactor catching fire or exploding.

The two sides argued through the day. If the danger of a fire or an explosion inside the reactor was real, an evacuation of the population was essential. Governor Thornburgh decided to trust the assessment given by Denton and his team of scientists.

None of this dispute over the possible danger of an explosion was announced to the news media, and neither Denton nor Thornburgh mentioned it in the news conference on Saturday evening.

———————

After dinner I drove back to my motel and tried once again to read the information booklet the Met Ed people had put out on the nuclear reactor. If I had come to some sort of hazy grasp about how the nuclear plant on Three Mile Island functioned, or at least was supposed to function, I still didn't understand it fully. I got into bed and opened the manual. But it was tough going. I didn't even know the meaning of half the words. I was trying to keep straight the difference between control rods and fuel rods, fission and fusion, rads and rems, feedwater and coolant when I began to nod off to sleep.

The telephone woke me with a jolt. One of the night editors

at U.P.I. headquarters in New York was calling. He said the A.P. had just moved a bulletin saying that there had been a sudden change in the bubble in the reactor, and that the scientists now had only hours instead of days to prevent a meltdown or a hydrogen explosion.

I was astounded. It had been only a couple of hours earlier that Denton assured everyone the bubble was stable and that they had days to get the reactor stabilized. And I had no idea what the editor in New York meant by the danger of an explosion.

"Who are they quoting?" I snapped back, suddenly very wide awake.

"It doesn't say," the editor told me. "All I have is the bulletin. The TV networks are breaking into their programming to announce it now."

"Are they quoting Denton?" I persisted. It was vital to have some idea of the source of the report in order to know how seriously to take it. "Is the story out of Pennsylvania?"

"Not Denton," the editor said. "Just 'informed sources.' But the bulletin is under a Washington dateline."

I tried to piece together what must have happened. It wasn't from Denton. It was somebody in Washington, and if it was an unnamed "informed source" it was somebody who was leaking information that he or she wanted to get out but did not want to take responsibility for. It sounded suspicious to me, especially after what Denton had said just a few hours earlier. However, things change quickly. If it was true, and there were only hours before a meltdown, then a general evacuation of a good part of southern Pennsylvania would be ordered immediately. It would be chaos.

"What does it say about an explosion?" I was baffled by that reference.

"You've got all I know," the editor said. "Do you want me to put out a story?"

"No!" I almost screamed. "At most put out an editor's advisory that we are checking 'unconfirmed reports.' Have you reached Hoop?"

"I called his home, but the line was busy. We have Washington working on it too."

The fact that Hoop's line was busy told me he was probably aware of the story and was trying to check it out. Maybe the Washington bureau could get something, since the story originated from there.

"Okay," I said. "I'm heading into the bureau. I'll call you from there. I'll try to reach Denton, but let us know what Washington finds out."

No sooner had I hung up than the phone rang again. It was Hoop.

"Have you heard?" he asked.

"I just got off the phone with New York. What have you found out?"

"Denton has called a news conference in half an hour at the state capitol."

"I'm on my way," I said. "I'll meet you there."

It didn't sound good. It was nearly midnight on a Saturday night and Denton was calling an urgent news conference. Maybe something had gone wrong. If so, this news conference could be to order an evacuation.

I took a quick look around the motel room. If there was an evacuation, I probably would not be coming back here. I thought about throwing some of my clothes in a bag, or at least grabbing my toothbrush. But there wasn't time. Was there anything I absolutely had to have besides the clothes on my back? The nuclear power plant handbook wouldn't be much help. I picked up my old portable typewriter that my parents had given me when I graduated from high school and ran to my car.

When I got to the state capitol it was just before midnight and the press room was as busy as on the opening day of the legislature. All the lights were on and forty or fifty reporters were talking on the phone, typing on typewriters, or trying to buttonhole state officials for information. Hoop, Sveilis, and DeLong were already there.

"Does anyone here know anything?" I asked.

"It seems to have caught everybody by surprise," Sveilis said. "Nobody is saying anything."

Suddenly there was a bustle of activity outside and a moment later Denton strode into the room with Governor Thornburgh. It was clear from the look on his face that Denton was not a happy man. He was scowling and slightly flushed and he went straight to the back of the room while reporters quickly gathered around him. He was clutching a sheet of paper. I noticed the paper in his hand was a piece of A.P. news copy.

He wasted no time. A report had been circulated, he said, claiming that there had been some sort of change in the size of the bubble and that there were only hours left to prevent a melt-down or an explosion in the reactor.

"This is not true," he said. He went on to categorically deny the story and to say again that there were days—not hours—to get rid of the bubble or even make a decision on an evacuation. He said the status of the bubble was still unchanged. He said there was no danger of an explosion. He called the report irresponsible.

When Denton finished, Governor Thornburgh announced that President Carter planned to make a visit to Three Mile Island for a personal inspection the next day. If I had any lingering doubts, that resolved them. The president of the United States wouldn't visit a nuclear power plant that was in danger of exploding at any minute. But whatever vindication we felt at being right was, I knew, cold comfort. The A.P. story would be in most newspapers the next day, and Denton's denial was too late to make most deadlines.

On my way back to the motel I saw dozens of cars filled with families, piled with luggage, heading out of town. The A.P. story, which had been reported on television, had scared a lot of people into abandoning their homes in the middle of the night.

CHAPTER 9

The idea to attend church services in Middletown that Sunday was not the greatest brainstorm I ever had. For one thing, just about every other reporter around Middletown, including the TV crews, had the same idea. For another, what we mostly found in church that Sunday was a lot of empty pews.

We had not realized just how many people around Middletown had already left. In fact, some churches canceled their services that Sunday altogether. I attended the early service at the local Presbyterian church, where some members of the congregation became upset when a TV crew started setting up its equipment, and the regular service at a Methodist church, where the minister took note of the out-of-town journalists in the congregation that morning and prayed in his benediction for "all those who have come to our town from far away to keep us informed of developments. . . even if their reports are contradictory." One member of the congregation shouted "Amen."

However, a measure of how frightened some of those residents who remained were came in the Roman Catholic service. The local priest had been authorized to give general absolution to all of his congregation that Sunday morning. This is a rite in the Catholic church that is given to people who face imminent death, such as soldiers about to go into battle.

But the main news that Sunday was the arrival of Jimmy Carter. On the surface, Carter's trip was aimed at easing the fears of those people who lived near the plant. If the president can walk around in the shadow of Three Mile Island, then it can't be all that dangerous. But Carter also wanted to discuss plans for a general evacuation of the entire area around Three Mile Island with Governor Thornburgh. Whether the reactor was potentially explosive or not, the possibility of a meltdown was still very real until the hydrogen bubble disappeared.

Covering an American president is always something of a three-ring circus. For one thing, a retinue of people sweeps in with him, to great fanfare. Then a bevy of secret service agents with wires hanging out of their ears surrounds the man himself so closely that you can hardly see him. Finally, a herd of reporters known as the White House press corps, follows him wherever he goes; for them there is no other story but what the president of the United States does and says.

But behind the scenes, this particular presidential visit also set the stage for a final showdown between the scientists in

There were more reporters than worshipers at many church services in Middletown on the Sunday following the accident.

64

CARTER VISITS NUCLEAR PLANT, URGES COOPERATION IN CRISIS; SOME EXPERTS VOICE OPTIMISM

Washington who feared the reactor could catch fire or explode at any moment and those on Three Mile Island, who saw no danger of an explosion and still believed they had days to eliminate the hydrogen bubble before a meltdown could occur.

Early that morning, Roger Mattson got into his car in Washington, D.C., and began driving toward Harrisburg. He wanted to arrive before the president, who, he was convinced, was heading into a volatile situation at Three Mile Island. Mattson reached the airport at the Pennsylvania capital just before the president and found Victor Stello, the chief nuclear engineer who was advising Harold Denton.

Even as the president's helicopter was landing, the two men were arguing inside the hangar at the airport over whether the reactor was about to catch fire or explode. Carter was given a briefing at Harrisburg airport by Denton, who faithfully reported both sides of the dispute. But Carter, who was a trained nuclear engineer and understood the situation better than most politicians, clearly trusted Denton; otherwise he wouldn't have come even as close as the Harrisburg airport. He decided to proceed with his tour of the crippled nuclear plant.

A crowd of about six hundred people turned out to greet Carter and his wife, Rosalynn, as they boarded an old yellow school bus and drove over the bridge to the island. The Carters, along with Governor Thornburgh, spent about half an hour on Three Mile Island. For the most part that segment of his visit was only a photo opportunity for press photographers. They put on bright yellow boots in case there were any puddles of radioactive water, and each wore a dosimeter to measure the amount of radiation they were receiving as they toured the control room.

All during the president's visit, Mattson and Stello were closeted in a small office, poring over the figures they had gotten from the plant's computers, trying to find out why they were reaching such different conclusions from the same data.

Finally Stello saw the flaw in Mattson's arguments. Mattson had been using an incorrect chemical formula. The radiolysis was not producing new oxygen that might trigger the hydrogen bubble. Some of the water in the reactor was indeed separating into hydrogen and oxygen molecules, but because there was so much extra hydrogen, the oxygen was constantly combining with it to form back into water. The bubble was, in effect, a built-in self-defense system against an explosion.

But the fact that the fear of an explosion had been unfounded did not mean that the danger of a meltdown had evaporated with it. The bubble itself was still there and it was still preventing water from reaching the tops of the fuel rods. The president told the governor that an evacuation might be necessary.

After his visit to the nuclear plant, Carter went to Middletown's town hall to meet with residents and hold a news conference. The local crowd cheered and applauded as the president

Harold Denton explained to President Carter why he felt a meltdown was not imminent.

66

walked in, but the message he gave them was not all that encouraging. He offered them his familiar smile, but his face looked drawn and worried, and when he spoke his voice had an edge of anxiety. He was not there to tell them their worries were over.

He said the situation at the plant was "stable" but there was still a danger and that residents might be asked to take "further steps." He did not say what those steps might be. He did not use the word "evacuation," but everyone knew that was what he meant.

After visiting the nuclear plant, President Carter spoke to local residents and reporters.

"I would like to say to the people who live around the Three Mile Island plant that if it does become necessary, Governor Thornburgh will ask you and others in this area to take appropriate action to insure your safety. If he does, I want to urge that these instructions be carried out calmly and exactly, as they have been in the past few days."

"If we make an error," the president said, "we want to err on the side of caution."

Then he was gone. As quickly as he had arrived in a bustling whirl of activity, he departed, leaving behind a sense of calm that was somehow not all that reassuring.

After the last of the limousines, secret service cars, and press buses pulled out of Middletown, Hoop and I looked at each other.

"What do you think about what he said?" Hoop asked.

"I think he just told everybody to pack their bags and gas up their cars," I replied.

CHAPTER 10

If the president's visit was intended as a gesture to put the residents of the towns and farms around Three Mile Island at ease, the general feeling around Middletown the following Monday morning was that unless something positive happened soon, an evacuation would be inevitable. Even Denton's estimate that the scientists had several days to get rid of the bubble before a meltdown began would soon return to haunt him.

This was now the sixth day since the accident, and what on Friday had seemed a comforting assurance had become an anxious reminder of the deadly peril that still existed as the "days" Denton said he had to cool the reactor ticked down into hours.

Denton had called a news conference for 11 A.M., and the popular opinion among reporters was that if Governor Thornburgh showed up with him it would be to order an evacuation. In fact, many of the reporters milling around the press center in Middletown were packed and ready to move out of town on short notice.

Sure enough, Governor Thornburgh was there. He entered first, but it was impossible to tell from his grim expression what he might be planning to announce. But I knew as soon as Denton walked into the room that if there was going to be an evacuation, it would not be that day. Denton was grinning from ear to ear.

Page 68.
The accident at Three Mile Island inspired grim humor among local residents, including the driver of this truck.

As with most news conferences, there was a brief statement and then a chance for reporters to ask questions. Denton made the opening statement that day. He began with the good news.

"There has been a dramatic decrease in the bubble size," he said proudly, like a brand-new father reporting to a waiting family that a baby has just been born after a difficult delivery.

Denton said that judging from all the data the scientists on Three Mile Island had collected, the bubble had shrunk to about fifty cubic feet in size. It had been as large as 1,000 cubic feet at one point. Most of the reduction had come overnight.

This meant, he said, that the coolant water that was being pumped into the reactor was reaching most of the fuel rods in the reactor's core. With the threat of a meltdown diminishing with each cubic foot that the bubble shrank, the necessity for a general evacuation was also growing more remote.

Governor Thornburgh announced that while there appeared now to be no imminent threat, he would keep an alert for possible evacuation in effect "as long as there is any conceivable risk." He also extended his order for all young children and pregnant women to remain at least five miles from the crippled reactor.

While clearly elated at this turn of events, Denton cautioned that the scientists were not out of the woods yet. The amount of radiation inside the containment building was still astronomically high, he said, with some readings running as high as 30,000 rems an hour—a rate so high that spending even a few minutes inside without protective clothing would be lethal for humans. He also said the scientists still had to bring the reactor to a complete shutdown, and he estimated that it would be years before the building could be decontaminated.

This was big news. Hoop raced to the telephone to get the story on the wire. Denton's news conference had been the first piece of good news for the area's residents since the crisis began, and I thought I would talk to some of the people who had remained throughout.

As I drove along the banks of the Susquehanna toward Three

Mile Island, the giant towers again loomed before me. They were almost mesmerizing, and I could hardly take my eyes off them.

The stretch of highway that runs past the nuclear plant is called River Road, and several houses were built on the side of the road, facing the river and the island. I couldn't imagine having that view out your living room window day after day.

Just as I was coming up on the entrance to the bridge that led from River Road across to the nuclear plant, I saw a general store off to the left with two cars in front. While most of the houses I had passed on the drive down had looked deserted, the store was clearly open and in business. Boyer's grocery store was, in effect, just across the street from the nuclear plant. I parked and went in.

It was one of those old-fashioned mom-and-pop stores that sell everything from canned soup to shoelaces, fishing lures to salami. George Boyer, who ran the store with his wife, Helen, dispensed homespun philosophy across the counter. In another day, there would have been a potbellied stove and a cracker barrel.

Boyer was waiting on a customer when I went in. I strolled around the store, jotting down a few observations in my notebook, then got a candy bar and went up to pay. As it turned out, Boyer, who said he was seventy-six, was eager to talk about the accident across the street, or just about anything else one cared to discuss.

The Boyers were one of only three families living along River Road who hadn't evacuated. He said his main concern over the nuclear accident was whether he should still plant his vegetable garden of carrots and tomatoes and onions that spring.

"Now I'm only concerned about any radiation that might have gotten into the ground," Boyer said. "They say it stays in the ground for a thousand years. Of course, I won't be around that long."

Boyer and his wife had lived in the Middletown area for forty-five years—they had moved there the same year they married. He and his wife had lived through two floods and one

George Boyer's general store was across the river from Three Mile Island.

General Store Philosopher Takes N-Crisis In Stride

By WILBORN HAMPTON

MIDDLETOWN, Pa. (UPI) — For George Boyer, there are more things in life to worry about than a nuclear accident across the street.

At 76, Boyer is something of a philosopher. His general store is located just across the street from the bridge that leads to Three Mile Island and its crippled nuclear plant. He also has learned to differentiate between what might have happened and what happened.

He said his motto is to take things as they come.

"As one gets older, life sometimes seems to get more complex," Boyer said. "But if you don't take it as it comes, you're in trouble."

Boyer and his wife were among only three families along River Road, the road that runs along the Susquehanna River at Three Mile Island, who stayed after the accident at the nuclear power plant.

"My wife started to worry a bit. But by the time we found out about it, it had been about six hours and I thought to myself, 'why bother leaving now?'"

Boyer said he was asleep when the first malfunction at Three Mile Island released deadly radiation about 4 a.m. on March 28. Some described the noise as sounding like a jet plane taking off, but it did not wake Boyer, who lives about 400 yards away.

"I'm about 50 percent deaf," he said. "I didn't hear about it until about 10 a.m. that morning. If anything was going to happen to me, I figured it had already happened by then.

Despite the furor generated by America's worst nuclear accident and the growing debate over the peril nuclear power poses to the population, Boyer is still convinced it is necessary.

"I was for it all along, thought it was a good idea," Boyer said. "They ought to fix that plant and turn it back on.

"Where else are we going to get our energy for the future," he said. "We won't use coal and can't afford oil. Until they find something else, we have to have nuclear energy.

"My wife's people used to work in coal mines over in Fayette County," he said. "They ran out of coal over there and everybody had to find new jobs. I said then we had to have a new source of power. I still agree with it.

During the years of building the nuclear plant, Boyer's store was a hangout for the hundreds of construction workers.

"I got to know a lot about it just from listening to them," he said. "They would come in here and drink a soda or whatever and talk. I got to know them and know about what was going on over there.

"I remember everything went real smooth on No. 1 — no problems at all," he said. "But No. 2 (the reactor that malfunctioned), there were always problems."

hurricane and he said it would take more than a nuclear accident to make them leave.

"My wife started to worry a bit at first," Boyer said. "But by the time we found out about it, it had been about six hours and I thought to myself, 'Why bother leaving now?' Besides I'd have to find some place to go where I could take the animals." He indicated two cats—Snoopy and Tony—who clearly had the run of the store. One was up on a top shelf among the canned peas. The other was curled near the cash register, keeping an eye on the customers.

"You know, some people just packed up and took off," Boyer said. "Left their dogs and cats behind. That's how scared they were. That's inhuman. Selfish. Humans can usually take care of themselves. Sometimes. But those poor animals . . . left alone."

During the years of the building of the plant, Boyer's store had been a hangout for the construction workers.

"I got to know a lot about it just from listening to them," he said. "They would come in here and drink a soda or whatever and talk. I got to know them and know about what was going on over there. I remember everything went real smooth on Unit No. 1. No problems at all. But No. 2—there were always problems."

Boyer said the construction of the nuclear plant had divided local residents from the start, although he and his wife had supported it and still do.

"I was for it all along," he said. "Thought it was a good idea. Where else are we going to get our energy for the future? We won't use coal and can't afford oil. Until they find something else we have to have nuclear energy. It's not so much for me. I won't be around that long. But these young kids are going to have to have it. They ought to fix that plant and turn it back on. You've got to go on. You can't keep worrying about what's going to happen next."

———————

Denton had called his next news conference for Tuesday afternoon, which meant we all had one more anxious night of waiting. At dinner that evening with Hoop and Sveilis and the other U.P.I. reporters there was a sense of relief, but it was a sort of nervous relief, like your team had just scored a go-ahead run in the top of the ninth inning but the opposing team still had one more turn at bat.

Residents began to return to the streets of Goldsboro, despite its proximity to the stricken plant.

I was never very good at waiting, so the next morning I decided to drive back over to Goldsboro and see if the ghost town had come back to life. It was a dull, cloudy day with a slight drizzle falling as I made the drive to the little town just across the Susquehanna from the giant towers.

There were no traffic jams in Goldsboro on Tuesday. But there were some cars parked on the main street. Several stores that had been closed on Saturday were now open. The post office was back in business, and a German shepherd dog was tied to the railing on the front porch. Reeser's grocery store was still shut, but the dining room at the King's Arms bar was serving meals that day for the first time in a week. The gas station was pumping gas again. Two teenage girls pedaled bicycles down the sidewalk toward the river, and several people were on the street. I parked the car and got out.

Ron Miller was wearing a green baseball cap and a yellow windbreaker against the early spring rain. He said several townspeople had returned Monday afternoon after the news about the reduction in the size of the bubble. Miller said he had stayed in the town through the crisis. "I would have left if they had ordered an evacuation," he said. "We had everything ready to go."

Miller said he had originally been opposed to the construction of the nuclear plant on the island across the river. But now that it had been built, he said, "They ought to repair it and turn it back on."

"We've all gotten over being scared—especially after this," Miller said. "I wouldn't move out now because of it. But I don't think I'd come here if I knew about it."

Driving back out of town I passed the house with the "Worms for Sale" sign in the front yard. The cardboard "Closed" sign was still attached and the house looked deserted. And with the knowledge that radioactive material had spilled out of the reactor on Three Mile Island, I didn't think many people would be fishing along the banks of that particular stretch of the Susquehanna for a long time to come.

———————

Once again, from the first moment I saw Harold Denton I knew there was good news. He strode into the afternoon news conference with the confidence of a man who has just awakened from a nightmare and realizes it was only a dream.

"Today I want to report that we consider the hydrogen bubble no longer a significant problem in this plant," he said.

Harold Denton was an instant hero to the residents of southern Pennsylvania, and received this letter of thanks from schoolchildren in Middletown.

Although he went on to say that the crisis would not officially be over until the reactor was brought to a cold shutdown, and Governor Thornburgh kept in force his order for pregnant women and young children to stay five miles away from the plant, Denton's statement that day was like a benediction for the residents of the area.

The threat of a meltdown had evaporated along with the bubble.

During the question period reporters were already turning to the future, asking what plans were being made to start the plant up again. Denton estimated that it would be four years before the plant could be back in operation.

Certainly the story in Pennsylvania was over for me. Later that afternoon, Steve told me to return to New York the next day. And if I had any doubts about whether the celebration was premature, they were dispelled when I saw a boy wearing a T-shirt that said: "I Survived Three Mile Island."

Three Mile Island Drama Plays To World Audience

By WILBORN HAMPTON

MIDDLETOWN (UPI) — Only a pale sliver of a new moon peeped through the dark clouds.

On an island in the middle of the Susquehanna River, a small group of men worked in a brilliantly lit control room, carefully monitoring walls of highly sensitive equipment. In the middle of the room was Harold Denton.

The men, some of the finest nuclear minds in the United States, did not like what they saw. Their equipment, like the moon outside, shed only a veiled light on what was happening in the heart of the Three Mile Island No. 2 nuclear power plant.

The walls filled with red, yellow, white — and occasionally green — lights offered little in the way of inspiration, illumination or imagination to tell what those men should do to protect half a million frightened people outside.

"They are way out in an unknown land," Prof. Henry Kendall of the Massachusetts Institute of Technology, a nuclear critic, said later of the men who had to face the crisis at Three Mile Island. "They are like children playing in the woods."

We all went to dinner that evening at a restaurant in Harrisburg. By coincidence, Harold Denton was at the same restaurant, at a table with three other people. He hardly got to eat a bite, however, for all the residents coming up to him to shake his hand and thank him. As he had been throughout the crisis, he was gracious and friendly. He put down his fork, stood, and chatted a bit with each well-wisher who stopped by his table. America had found a hero that week.

After dinner, the entire U.P.I. crew went to the bar that had become the journalist hangout in Harrisburg for a farewell drink. As we left, I noticed the little blackboard where the weather forecast was chalked. It read, "Partly cloudy with a 40% chance of survival."

The laughter came a little easier that Tuesday night. We had all survived Three Mile Island.

A T-shirt heralded the good news.

CHERNOBYL

APRIL 26, 1986

CHAPTER **11**

By the end of the week Three Mile Island was off the front pages. Journalists looked elsewhere for their headlines and the public at large lost interest in the disaster that didn't happen. Yet the horrifying prospect of what might have occurred never entirely went away.

For the next few years the debate heated up on whether the United States should continue to promote nuclear power as the energy of the future, and the near catastrophe in Pennsylvania figured prominently in it. Three Mile Island had made a lot of ordinary citizens very wary of nuclear energy.

Then one spring night, seven years and twenty-nine days after the accident at Three Mile Island, an explosion and fire broke out at a Soviet nuclear power station called Chernobyl, in the Ukraine. Just about everything that didn't happen at Three Mile Island happened at Chernobyl.

Page 80.
At Chernobyl a fire and explosion
spewed large amounts of radiation
into the atmosphere and reduced
parts of Unit No. 4 to rubble.

Just like the one at Three Mile Island, the accident at Chernobyl began during the overnight shift. And like Craig Faust and Ed Frederick at Unit No. 2 at Three Mile Island, Alexander Nekhayev was an engineer on duty in the control room of Unit No. 4 of the Chernobyl power station. At 1:23 A.M. on April 26, 1986, Nekhayev was sitting in front of the control panel when he felt a sudden jolt. "It was like somebody had pushed my chair," he said later. The reactor inside the power plant had exploded.

Alarms went off and lights began flashing on the control board. The explosion blew the roof off the top of the reactor and ignited a fire. Technicians began to call fire departments in all the nearby towns, but within minutes it became clear that the fire inside the reactor was out of control. An emergency call was made to Kiev, the capital of the Ukraine, about seventy miles to the south, asking for help in battling the blaze.

The telephone operator in Kiev asked how many firemen they needed.

"Everybody," the technician in Chernobyl replied. "Send everybody."

Within an hour, an army of firefighters converged on the plant. But none of them had special training in fighting a nuclear reactor fire. "We did not know anything," Petz Hmil, one of the first firemen to reach the scene, said later. "We had been told a nuclear reactor could not explode."

Although the U.S. and Soviet reactors were of significantly different designs, the Soviet technicians at Chernobyl—just like the technicians at Three Mile Island—did not know what had happened to cause the explosion and fire, and they did not know what to do to stop the disaster that was by now on a roller coaster toward catastrophe.

By dawn, the firemen had brought most of the flames in Unit No. 4 under control. But the core of the reactor, which was open to the air, was still ablaze. Plant officials ordered the firemen to train streams of water onto it. After all, that is the way one fights most fires—with water. But this was the worst thing they could have done. The instant the water hit the molten core of the reactor it turned into radioactive steam, which formed into clouds that rose into the atmosphere to be carried whichever way the wind blew. The deadly fallout from Chernobyl had begun.

At first the Soviet authorities, just like the Met Ed officials at Three Mile Island, tried to pretend nothing was wrong.

Chernobyl was located about two miles from Pripyat, a new town that had been built to accommodate the workers at the nuclear plant. And no one in Pripyat knew anything had happened at the nuclear plant. The accident occurred on a Saturday, and children played outdoors and their mothers did the shopping. Some of the off-duty workers had been called to the plant to deal with "an emergency," but they weren't told what was wrong.

The first hint the town had of the possible disaster came later that day, when truckloads of men wearing gas masks and protective clothing showed up in Pripyat and began to spray foam on the streets. There were other signs that something had happened at the plant: scores of helicopters flew over the town in the direction of Chernobyl throughout the day, and the sale of fresh vegetables at the outdoor market was abruptly halted by government officials. Still, residents were allowed to go about their business as though nothing unusual had occurred.

On the second day after the accident the people of Pripyat awoke to the sound of loudspeaker trucks alerting them that the entire town would be evacuated within hours. They were told to take only enough clothes to last for two days. Scores of buses arrived in the town. Children went first. They were ordered onto the buses, many with only the clothes on their backs and without any idea where they were going. They were driven to Kiev and other towns south of Pripyat. Some children were separated from their parents, and neither adults nor children knew where they were being taken. Even then, the residents of Pripyat were not told that anything was wrong at the nuclear plant.

But the Soviet Union would not be able to keep Chernobyl a secret much longer. Winds were carrying the fallout from the burning reactor farther and farther north. The first hint from the outside that something terrible had happened came from Sweden. Workers at a power plant near Stockholm recorded increased radiation there. At first they thought something was wrong at their own plant. Then they began to calculate the direction and velocity of the wind and soon realized they were getting radiation that was coming from somewhere in the Ukraine. The Swedish government demanded an explanation, but the Soviet Union still denied any accident had occurred.

But the Swedish report alerted the rest of the world. Finally, Soviet television reported there had been an incident at one of their nuclear plants. But just as the Met Ed officials in Pennsylvania had done, the Soviet authorities said the situation was "under control."

However, the burning nuclear core at Chernobyl kept emitting radioactivity into the atmosphere, and every time the wind changed it carried the fallout in a different direction. Over the

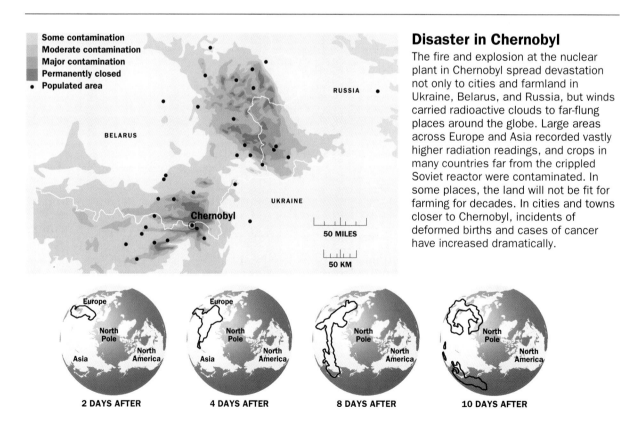

Disaster in Chernobyl

The fire and explosion at the nuclear plant in Chernobyl spread devastation not only to cities and farmland in Ukraine, Belarus, and Russia, but winds carried radioactive clouds to far-flung places around the globe. Large areas across Europe and Asia recorded vastly higher radiation readings, and crops in many countries far from the crippled Soviet reactor were contaminated. In some places, the land will not be fit for farming for decades. In cities and towns closer to Chernobyl, incidents of deformed births and cases of cancer have increased dramatically.

next few days, increased radiation readings were recorded across Europe to the west and in Siberia to the east. An estimated 260,000 people were evacuated from towns within a twenty-mile radius around Chernobyl. At one point plans were discussed to evacuate the entire population of Kiev, a city of nearly 3 million people. But the winds changed again and those plans were dropped.

Still the Chernobyl core burned, spewing radioactivity into the atmosphere.

Soviet officials decided they would have to do something to try to extinguish the glowing core of the reactor. Thousands of Soviet Army soldiers and workers began to fill sacks with lead and sand that were then loaded onto helicopters and dropped into the core. Local residents, none of whom wore protective clothing, were pressed into service to help fill the sacks. This went on for days, but in the end it had little effect. Still the reactor's core burned.

Then the Soviet technicians learned that they faced an even greater threat. The core was in danger of melting down to the ground water level, which would create the ultimate "China syndrome" catastrophe.

An estimated 10,000 miners from all parts of the Soviet Union were flown in to tunnel beneath the crippled reactor and fill in the ground beneath it with tons of cement to provide an extra layer of protection between the molten fuel and the water table.

By the middle of May, two weeks after the explosion and fire, Soviet officials decided they would have to encase Unit No. 4 completely, to protect the environment from radiation emissions. Tens of thousands of Soviet Army troops joined a special team of civilian workers to begin the dangerous task of building a concrete mausoleum around the reactor. The job took until November and at one time or another involved more than half a million workers from all across the Soviet Union, all of whom were exposed to the high levels of radiation being emitted from the burning core.

There is no official death toll for Chernobyl. At the time, the Soviet government reported that 31 people died in the accident. But since the breakup of the Soviet Union, more honest assessments of the extent of the tragedy have come out. The Ukraine, which is now an independent nation, has said that more than 4,300 people died there. Nearly all the firemen who battled the blaze that first night are now dead, most from cancer or other radiation-related illnesses. Petz Hmil has seen all of his colleagues die over the years since the accident. Deaths among the soldiers and workers who built the concrete shell around the reactor are estimated to number at least 6,000, but nobody knows for sure, since many of those who worked at Chernobyl returned to their homes far away.

The land around the Chernobyl plant is a wasteland. Ukrainian officials say that 160,000 square kilometers were contaminated with radioactive fallout at a level forty times greater than the level of radiation that Hiroshima or Nagasaki received from the first atomic bombs. That land will remain contaminated for decades, possibly as long as a hundred years.

The people who left their homes in Pripyat on a couple of hours notice in 1986 have never returned. Pripyat is now a ghost town, its streets a graveyard for trucks and helicopters that had to be abandoned because they were so covered with radioactive dust. Bulldozers have buried most of the houses, and the old apartment blocks are deserted, the possessions of the former inhabitants too radioactive to reclaim. The residents of Pripyat lost everything they owned.

But the calamity did not end with the sealing off of the melted reactor core. People are still dying as a result of illnesses caused by radiation. According to the World Health Organization, the number of thyroid cancer cases among children in the region is one hundred times higher than it was before the accident. The rate of leukemia, which begins to show up about ten years after severe exposure to radiation, is also increasing rapidly among children throughout the region.

Ten years after the disaster at Chernobyl, Pripyat, the nearby city in which 40,000 people once lived, is now deserted.

Al Many is a rural community about 120 miles west of Chernobyl. All but four of the two hundred school-age children in the town are now ill with some form of radiation sickness. Farmers can grow nothing on their land.

In Gomel, a town about sixty miles north of Chernobyl that received perhaps the heaviest concentration of radioactive fallout, the local orphanage is full of infants and young children as a result of what has become an epidemic of birth defects among babies now being born to women who received large doses of radiation.

Nina Belskaya is one of the doctors who try to help these abandoned children. But she sees a future that is fraught only with fear. "We are afraid the reactor will explode again and kill us all," she said. "We are afraid our children's children will be born unhealthy. We are afraid of everything."

Chernobyl has become a nightmare from which its victims never wake. As Andrei Serdyuk, the Ukrainian health minister, said in an interview, "Chernobyl will be with us forever."

In the end, the damaged reactors at Three Mile Island and Chernobyl shared a similar fate. Both ended up as concrete-covered mausoleums. Harold Denton was overly optimistic when he said it would be four years before Three Mile Island could be working again. It was four years before scientists could send even a robot with a camera into the Unit No. 2 core to inspect the damage. The pictures showed that nearly half of the reactor's fuel rods were damaged, meaning that it had suffered at least a partial meltdown. That meant that some twenty tons of molten uranium fuel had flowed to the bottom of the reactor. It was another two years before workers could finally begin removing the damaged fuel rods, and the full decontamination process took eight more years after that. Unit No. 2 will never produce electricity again.

Although there were many differences between the types of reactors and between what happened at Three Mile Island and what took place at Chernobyl, the two accidents were a major setback for those who still believe nuclear energy is the way of the future. After all, no one wants to carry a geiger counter on every trip to the grocery store just to measure the radiation in the food. And no one wants to increase the possibility that children might be born with horrible deformities or face early death from cancer.

Not a single new nuclear reactor has been ordered anywhere in the United States since the accident at Three Mile Island. And since Chernobyl, one after another of the countries in Europe has decided against building more atomic energy plants.

But existing nuclear plants still provide electricity in parts of the United States, Europe, and elsewhere around the world. The other reactors at the Chernobyl complex, for example, continued to operate for years after the accident, although the staff and technicians who worked there had to live at least twenty miles away and were bused in to their jobs every day. It was only after the United States and other European nations agreed to pay the Ukraine millions of dollars in compensation that the

Ukraine promised to completely shut down the Chernobyl reactors by 2001.

Since the accidents at Three Mile Island and Chernobyl, people have become more jittery about the use of technology to produce nuclear energy. Every time there is a hiccup at a nuclear plant, the whole world seems to hold its breath.

As the century that gave us atomic energy drew to a close, a small accident in Japan rekindled the fear of nuclear energy all Japanese struggle to contain. Because Japan suffered the horrors of two atomic bombings during World War II, its people are perhaps even more sensitive than those of other nations to the anxieties inherent in nuclear power.

The accident occurred on September 30, 1999, as workers were mixing nuclear fuel at the Sumitomo Metal Mining Company, about eighty-five miles northwest of Tokyo. They poured too much uranium into a tank of nitric acid, which set off a chain reaction that raced out of control. The reaction set off a huge flash of blue light and sent plumes of radiation shooting into the air like geysers.

A total of 35 people were exposed to excessive amounts of radiation, and 300,000 people who lived within a six-mile radius

Health authorities in the Ukraine discourage citizens from buying vegetables from street vendors as they may have been grown in areas contaminated by radiation from Chernobyl.

of the plant were ordered to stay indoors. The chain reaction was brought under control within a day, but it reopened the closet of fears that the Japanese try to keep locked shut. But they and people around the world, from Three Mile Island to Chernobyl, live with those fears never far from their minds.

———————

Despite the potential for disaster that came so close at Three Mile Island, and that was realized at Chernobyl, nuclear energy still has many supporters. For one thing, no one has found a successful and affordable alternative source of energy to replace our reliance on coal and other fossil fuels. The fact remains that the world's supply of oil could run out sometime in the twenty-first century. And not only is there a limited supply of coal, but it is also harmful to the environment. The debate on the use of nuclear energy is far from over. Many scientists are still convinced that the atom offers the best solution for the growing energy needs of the world. The final verdict on nuclear energy will eventually be given by the children of today.

For once we have burned up all our oil and coal and forests, it is today's youth who will have to reinvent a world that depends more and more on electricity. Perhaps some child in a classroom somewhere today will be the one who finds a better way to harness the wind or an economical way to bottle the sun's energy. Or perhaps, he or she will discover a safer way to convert the enormous power contained in the tiny atom into service for humankind.

ACKNOWLEDGMENTS

This book would not have been completed without the valued assistance of many people. First and foremost is Dr. Alan J. Friedman, director of the New York Hall of Science, who generously shared his considerable knowledge of the behavior of atoms and attempted against all odds to explain to me the fundamentals of nuclear physics. Any errors of science that remain in the book are through no fault of his and merely provide further evidence of why I failed physics in college. Mary Pope Osborne and Will Osborne offered much-appreciated suggestions along the way. The faith of my editors, Amy Ehrlich and Gale Pryor, sustained me through difficult times and enabled me to complete the project, and the clarity of vision of Sherry Fatla has given the book its dramatic design. In addition to Bill Hoop and my former U.P.I. colleagues, I am further indebted to the countless journalists around the world who have covered the story of atomic energy from Hiroshima and Three Mile Island to Chernobyl and beyond. Finally, as with any endeavor I undertake, my main source of strength is my wife, LuAnn Walther.

Chain reaction: When the nuclei of uranium atoms split, they emit neutrons that split other uranium atoms in a continuing process.

Coolant: The fluid, usually water, that carries the heat caused by the nuclear chain reaction away from the core of the reactor.

Core: The part of a reactor that contains the nuclear fuel rods.

Critical mass: The stage at which the number of neutrons being emitted in a chain reaction becomes sufficient to keep the process going.

Fallout: The radioactive particles that rain down on an area or that are carried by the wind following a nuclear accident or explosion.

Fission: The splitting of the nuclei of atoms in a chain reaction; the energy released from the fission is what provides the heat that eventually becomes electricity.

Fuel rods: Stainless steel tubes that contain pellets of uranium or other nuclear fuel used to make the chain reaction.

Fusion: The release of nuclear energy by the bonding, or fusing, of atomic nuclei like hydrogen. It is the opposite of fission, which gets its energy by splitting the atomic nuclei.

Meltdown: A catastrophic event in a nuclear plant. It occurs when the fuel rods containing the uranium pellets melt from overheating. This happens when the core of a reactor loses the coolant water that keeps its temperature within controllable limits. In a meltdown, the nuclear rods burn through the reactor and containment building and seep into the ground, releasing massive amounts of radioactivity.

Rad: Stands for "radiation absorbed dose," a term that is commonly used to measure the amount of radiation taken in by a human being. A millirad is one-thousandth of a rad. There is considerable difference of opinion over how many millirads are safe for humans to receive.

Radiation sickness: The range of illnesses that come from over-exposure to radioactivity; symptoms include weakness, fatigue, loss of appetite, vomiting, diarrhea, uncontrolled bleeding, and the collapse of the immune system, which can lead to serious diseases. If the amount of radiation to which a person is exposed is heavy enough, it can cause brain damage and death.

Radioactivity: The spontaneous disintegration of the nucleus of an atom, such as uranium, with the emission of radiation. This energy radiates outward in the form of particles or rays, such as alpha, beta, and gamma rays. Gamma rays are more penetrating than other forms of radiation.

Reactor: The core and its container shell, sometimes called a vessel.

Rem: Stands for "roentgen equivalent man." It is the measure of gamma ray radiation that is absorbed by humans. One rem has the same biological effect on humans as one rad. Most measurements are in millirems, or thousandths of a rem. The average American receives 100 to 200 millirems of radiation a year, from X-rays to cosmic rays.

Uranium: A chemical element. A metal with radioactive properties, it is often used as fuel in nuclear reactors because of its ability to undergo continuous fission.

Alternative Energy Sources by Gary Chandler and Kevin Graham
(Henry Holt & Co. 1996)

The American Experience: Meltdown at Three Mile Island at www.pbs.org

Chernobyl and Other Nuclear Accidents (New Perspectives) by Judith Condon
(Raintree Steck-Vaughn 1999)

Energy (Dorling Kindersley Eyewitness Books) by Jack Challoner, photographs by
Clive Streetcar (Dorling Kindersley 2000)

Hiroshima by John Hersey (Knopf hc 1985), (Vintage pb 1989)

Hiroshima and Nagasaki by Jane Claypool (F. Watts 1984)

Hiroshima no pika by Toshi Maruki (Lothrop, Lee & Shepard books 1982)

The Legacy of Chernobyl by Zhores A. Medvedev (W. W. Norton & Co. 1992)

The New Way Things Work by David Macaulay (Houghton Mifflin 1998)

Nuclear Energy by Gini Holland (Benchmark Press 1996)

Pass the Energy, Please! by Barbara Shaw McKinney, illustrated by Chad Wallace
(Dawn Publications 2000)

Quarks and Sparks: The Story of Nuclear Power by J. S. Kidd and Renee A. Kidd
(Facts on File, Inc. 1999)

Sadako and the Thousand Paper Cranes by Eleanor Coerr, illustrated by
Ronald Himler (Puffin 1999)

Blair, Ian. *Taming the Atom: Facing the Future with Nuclear Power.* Bristol, England: Adam Hilger, 1983.

D'Antonio, Michael. *Atomic Harvest: Hanford and the Lethal Toll of America's Nuclear Arsenal.* New York, NY: Crown Publishers, 1993.

Ford, Daniel F. *Three Mile Island: Thirty Minutes to Meltdown.* New York, NY: Penguin Books, 1982.

Gould, Jay M., and Benjamin A. Goldman. *Deadly Deceit: Low Level Radiation and High Level Cover-Up.* New York, NY: Four Walls Eight Windows, 1990.

Hersey, John. *Hiroshima.* New York, NY: Vintage Books edition, 1989.

The Union of Concerned Scientists. *Safety Second: The NRC and America's Nuclear Power Plants.* Bloomington, IN: Indiana University Press, 1987.

Williams, Robert C., and Philip L. Cantelon. *The American Atom.* Philadelphia, PA: University of Pennsylvania Press, 1984.

ALAMOGORDO, N.Mex., site of first atomic explosion, 3

AL MANY, village near Chernobyl, 87

ASSOCIATED PRESS (A.P.), 15, 59, 61

ATOMIC BOMB, first bombs dropped on Japan, 3–5, 91

BELSKAYA, Nina, doctor in Gomel, 87

BOYER, George, grocer across from Three Mile Island, 71–73

CALLAHAN, John, worker at Three Mile Island, 24

CARTER, Jimmy, President of the United States, 31, 61
   visit to Three Mile Island, 64–67

CHERNOBYL, Soviet nuclear plant, accident and meltdown, 81–92
   effects of accident on children, 86–87
   estimates of death toll, 86
   fallout from, 83, 84, 85
   soldiers and miners dig tunnel, 85

CHINA SYNDROME, THE, movie about a nuclear meltdown, 30, 85

DeLONG, Ed, U.P.I. reporter, 47, 60

DENTON, Harold, presidential representative at Three Mile Island, 31, 37–38, 47, 49, 52–55, 58–61, 69–70, 73, 75–77, 90

ENOLA GAY, B-29 bomber that dropped first atomic bomb, 4, 5

FAUST, Craig, worker at Three Mile Island, 22, 23

FREDERICK, Ed, worker at Three Mile Island, 22, 23

GOLDSBORO, town across from plant, 41–45, 74–75

GOMEL, town near Chernobyl, 87

GROTEVANT, Bob, U.P.I. reporter, 47, 55

HARRISBURG, PA., state capital, 21, 65, 77

HENDRIE, Joseph M., N.R.C. chairman, 51, 57

HIROSHIMA, Japanese city destroyed by first atomic bomb, 4–5, 10, 11, 86

HMIL, Petz, Soviet fireman at Chernobyl, 82, 86

HOOP, William, U.P.I. Harrisburg bureau manager, 18, 21, 22, 29, 31, 35, 38, 39, 46, 47, 54, 55, 60, 67, 70, 73

HOUSER, Ed, chemist at Three Mile Island, 25, 27

JONES, Ron, Goldsboro resident, 43

KIEV, capital of Ukraine, 82, 85

LAWRENCE, William, *New York Times* reporter, 3

LITTLE BOY, name of first atomic bomb, 4

LOGAN, Walter, U.P.I. foreign editor, 16, 19

MacLEOD, Scott, U.P.I. reporter, 47, 55

MATTSON, Roger, government scientist, 50, 58
   dispute with Victor Stello, 65–66

MELTDOWN, 31

METROPOLITAN EDISON, owner of Three Mile Island plant, 22–23, 83, 84
    denies danger at plant, 24–27
    vents radioactivity from plant, 29

MIDDLETOWN, closest large town to plant, 29, 39, 69
    church services in, 63–64
    many residents evacuate, 33
    food shortages, 33–34
    visit by President Carter, 66

MILLER, Gary, manager at Three Mile Island plant, 24

MILLER, Ron, Goldsboro resident, 74

MILLER, Woodrow, Goldsboro resident, 44

NAGASAKI, Japanese city that was target of second atomic bomb, 4, 10, 86

NEKHAYEV, Alexander, nuclear engineer at Chernobyl, 82

NEW YORK TIMES, 3, 17

NUCLEAR POWER, peaceful uses of, 9–10
    debate on safety of, 10–11
    first power plant built, 11
    future of nuclear power, 90–92

NUCLEAR REGULATORY COMMISSION (N.R.C.), 24, 50, 51

PRIPYAT, town near Chernobyl, 83, 86
    evacuation of, 83

SERDYUK, Andrei, Ukrainian health minister, 87

SHIPPINGPORT, Pa., site of first U.S. nuclear power plant, 11

SOVIET UNION, race to build atomic weapons, 8
    initial denial of nuclear accident, 83
    television report on Chernobyl, 84

STELLO, Victor, nuclear engineer, 58
    dispute with Roger Mattson, 65–66

STEVENSON, H. L. executive editor of U.P.I., 16–19, 22, 47, 76

SUMITOMO METAL MINING COMPANY, nuclear accident at, 91

SUSQUEHANNA RIVER, 22, 70

SVEILIS, Emil, U.P.I. reporter, 22, 46, 47, 55, 60, 61 73

THOMPSON, Dudley, official from Nuclear Regulatory Commission, 30

THORNBURGH, Richard, governor of Pennsylvania, 37, 51, 58, 64–67, 69, 70, 76
    orders evacuation of schoolchildren and pregnant women and closes schools, 32

THREE MILE ISLAND, Pennsylvania nuclear plant, 11, 15, 21, 69, 77, 81, 90
    accident at plant, 16–18, 22–27
    compared to Chernobyl, 82, 90–92
    general emergency declared, 24
    partial meltdown, 90
    President Carter's visit to, 64–67

UKRAINE, former Soviet republic where Chernobyl was built, 81, 84, 86, 87

UNITED PRESS INTERNATIONAL (U.P.I.), 15, 59, 73, 77

WORLD HEALTH ORGANIZATION, report on Chernobyl victims, 86

DIAGRAMS AND MAPS copyright © 2001 by Sean McNaughton